HEALING THE HOLES IN MY SOUL!

How I Saved My Own Life, Became Whole to Lead a Happy, Fulfilling and Joyous Life!

Rev. ORESTE J. D'AVERSA

PUBLISHER'S NOTE

This book is designed to provide accurate and authoritative information in regard to the subject matter covered. It is sold with the understanding that neither the author nor publisher is engaged in rendering psychological, legal or other professional service. If psychological, legal, professional advice or other expert assistance is required, the services of a professional, in that field, should be sought. The principles and concepts presented in this book are the opinions of the author and based on his interpretations of the aforementioned principles. Neither the author nor publisher are liable or responsible to any person or entity for any errors contained on this book, website, or for any special, incidental, or consequential damage caused or alleged to be caused directly or indirectly by the information contained in this book or website. Any application of the techniques, ideas and suggestions in this book is at the reader's sole discretion and risk.

Copyright © Oreste J. D'Aversa, 2020. All rights reserved.

No part of this publication may be reproduced, redistributed, taught, stored in a retrieval system, or transmitted, in any form or by any means, electronic, mechanical, photocopy, recording, or otherwise, without the prior written permission of the publisher.

FIRST EDITION

ISBN: 978-1-952294-00-6

Library of Congress Number: 20202902649 – Paramus, NJ

Published by: *Cutting Edge Technology Publishing.*

ANOTHER PUBLISHER'S NOTE

This book is not a substitute for trained medical and/or psychological help. If you have any type of thoughts, or concerns of suicide, or your mental health status regarding taking your own life consult a doctor, psychologist or other medical and mental health professionals. This book is meant to be used **"in addition to and not instead of"** working with trained medical, mental health and spiritual professionals. They will work with you and are a part of your healing team and healing journey. Call on them, they are there to be of service and to help you.

Are You or Someone You Love at Risk of Suicide? *

National Suicide Prevention Lifeline ™
1-800-273-8255
https://SuicidePreventionLifeline.org/

They can all help prevent suicide. The Lifeline provides 24/7, free and confidential support for people in distress, prevention and crisis resources for you or your loved ones, and best practices for professionals.

Suicide Warning Signs

- Threatening to hurt or kill oneself or talking about wanting to hurt or kill oneself.
- Feeling hopeless.
- Talking or writing about death, dying, suicide when these actions are out of the ordinary for the person.
- Withdrawing from friends, family, and society.
- Felling rage or uncontrolled anger or seeking revenge.
- Acting reckless or engaging in risky activities – seemingly without thinking.
- Feeling anxious, agitated, or unable to sleep or sleeping all the time. .
- Increasing alcohol or drug use.
- Looking for ways to kill oneself by seeking access to firearms, available pills, or other means.
- Feeling trapped – like there's no way out
- Experiencing dramatic mood changes.
- Seeing no reason for living or having no sense of purpose in life.

* U.S. Department of Health and Human Services
Substance Abuse and Mental Health Services Administration
www.samhsa.gov
Printed: September 2005 – CMHS-SVP-0126

DEDICATION

This book is dedicated to you (the reader).

If you are thinking about taking your own life, do your very best every day to overcome your thoughts and/or feelings of suicide.

Sometimes it may even be an hour-to-hour or minute-to-minute struggle. Help is available.

People are there for you who really want to help.

<u>They will make a difference in your life as you will one day make a difference in someone else's life.</u>

You're here for a very important purpose!

Find that purpose and live it!

Don't give up!

You matter to God, yourself and you matter to others!

NINE VERY IMPORTANT REASONS TO LIVE

1. You Came Here to Make a Difference

2. Live Out Your Life's Purpose

3. People Need You to Help Them

4. One Person Really Needs You and Only You Can Reach That One Person

5. Family - Especially if You Have Children

6. Friends and Acquaintances

7. The Next Generation Needs Your Guidance

8. The Animals Need Your Love and You Need Their Love as Well

9. God Needs You to Help Out on Earth
(and when God asks for something
it's always a good idea to do what God asks)

ACKNOWLEDGEMENT

My Faith in God

My faith in God has come to me by many trials and tribulations in my life. In the worst of circumstances when I thought all would be lost, in the very last moments of the 11th hour, God has rescued me, time and time again. There are no logical reasons for these rescues. A way was found for me where there appeared to be no way. I am human, and in being so, still doubt that God will be there for me when I need him/her. The fear is in my head and not in my soul. I know that God is never really far from me; as God is a part of me, and I am a part of God—as we all are. For all of God's love I will be forever grateful.

MORE ACKNOWLEDGEMENTS

I have also been blessed with the presence of Jesus the Christ and the Holy Spirit in my life, they have and continue to heal, help and guide me with their instructions, support and love.
I also want to acknowledge the continuing assistance of Archangel Michael, Archangel Gabrielle, Archangel Raphael, Archangel Uriel and other named and unnamed Seraphim Angels, my Spirit Guides and Guardians, all of which help me in ways I do not always know, understand or totally appreciate at times.
The support of all of my ancestors,
may they all find peace,
healing and love.
I am grateful to them all.

ABOUT THE AUTHOR

Rev. Oreste J. D'Aversa, or "Reverend Rusty" as he is known informally, is an Inter-Faith (All-Faiths) Minister ordained in the physical world by The New Seminary in New York City, New York; and ordained in the spiritual world by God the Father, God the Mother and Holy Spirit. Raised Catholic and having received the Sacraments of Baptism, Holy Communion, and Confirmation, Rev. D'Aversa follows the teachings of God, Jesus the Christ, The Holy Spirit, the Prophets, and the Ascended Masters.

He is here to serve God and humankind to help make the world a better place for all people. Reverend D'Aversa is an Author, Speaker, Spiritual Coach/Advisor and helps people by offering spiritual guidance, helping find their true life's purpose and living their true spiritual path. He is also a Business Coach, Consultant, Trainer and University Lecturer. He has appeared on radio and television as well as having his work featured in various newspapers and journals.

To learn more about him you can go to his websites
www.HealingHolesInMySoul.com
www.GodLovesYouAndMe.org
www.OresteDAversa.com

TABLE OF CONTENTS

Introduction 1

PART I: How I Got This Way...3
    Chapter 1: My Childhood 5

PART II: The Feeling's and Emotions.............................17
    Chapter 2: God, Where the Hell Were You!...................... 19
    Chapter 3: Your Feelings Will Wait.................................... 23
    Chapter 4: Pain is Pain, Just the Wrapper is Different 25
    Chapter 5: Loneliness, Lonely, Alone… 29
    Chapter 6: I'm Less Than.. 33
    Chapter 7: Pain, Anger and Sorrow 37
    Chapter 8: I Have Seen the Darkness – Many, Many Times...41
    Chapter 9: Depression 45
    Chapter 10: Shame 49
    Chapter 11: Rage!!! 53
    Chapter 12: Addiction – My Crutch to Never Healing 55
    Chapter 13: I Fooled the World but was Only
        Fooling Myself.. 57
    Chapter 14: Meet My Longtime Companion - Suicide 59

PART III: Recovery and Rebuilding................................63
    Chapter 15: Adulthood... 65
    Chapter 16: I'm Not Damaged or Broken 67
    Chapter 17: Breaking the Chains of Pain 69
    Chapter 18: Wholeness and "Hole-ness" 73

Chapter 19: Healing 77

Chapter 20: Forgiveness 85

Chapter 21: All You Need is Love 89

Chapter 22: The Animal Kingdom 91

Chapter 23: Mother Nature 93

Chapter 24: Gratitude 95

Chapter 25: The Spirituality of Suicide - The Spiritual Law
of Karma and Other Realities of Life Before Life 99

Chapter 26: Discovering Our Life's Purpose
– The Journey Within 109

Chapter 27: God Will Help Us 115

Conclusion: It's Not the End It's a New Beginning 119

Resources: Suicide Prevention Groups, Prayers,
Meditations, Exercises, Readings, Books 125

Footnotes 167

Bibliography 171

INTRODUCTION

As an Inter-Faith Minister (I prefer to use the term "All-Faiths Minister"), I started looking at the world one day and wondered why so many people are taking their own life. People well known and not so well known; people who on the outside look like they have it all but on the inside really did not have it all, but were empty and in pain (be it physical, mental, emotional, or spiritual), and the only way out was to take their own life.

It got me thinking about my own life as I too have reached that point, several times in my life, where I said it's just too hard to go on, it's just too much. Through God's grace I have endured and learned to "Heal the Holes" in my soul. Though I still have my "bad times," however not as bad as they once were, or don't last as long as they used to, or take me to the "poison" in my soul, I learned there are ways through the bad times – I don't have to be a victim anymore, or endure the emotional pain I did at the time.

This is my story, a man who went from having "Holes" in his soul to being "Whole" again. Whatever you are going through, don't give up. There is always hope, there is always God. God will find a way where there appears to be no way. God has not given up on you, so you don't give up on yourself.

I sincerely hope the tools in this book will be of help to you on your journey in this game we call life. This is my journey through the "pain, anger and sorrow" of my life. I healed the holes in my soul and so can you!

PART I

HOW I GOT THIS WAY

CHAPTER 1

My Childhood

I was born an only child to an immigrant Italian couple in Queens, New York in the late 1950's. They were both illiterate but managed to get by as most immigrants do in America. Neither one of my parents finished elementary school in their country, so they were not book smart. My father was a skilled laborer, as he was a bricklayer and stone mason, and my mother did some factory work and took care of the family. The classic immigrant story, coming to a foreign country, they worked hard and put food on the table for which I am proud of my parents and of my Italian heritage.

I will be saying many things in this book about my parents, most not good, but I loved both of them that's why it makes it extremely difficult to talk about how they both emotionally hurt me, intentionally or not intentionally, the "Pain, Anger and Sorrow" is present, nonetheless. It may sound like "I'm talking out of mouth sides of my mouth" ("I'm talking out of mouth sides of my mouth" – a New York City expression meaning I'm contradicting what I'm saying about a subject or person) about my parents, but things are never "black and white" when it comes to family. Family and family emotions are what they are, many times are neither logical or linear, and your feelings are <u>your feelings</u>. Many times, are very hurtful at that!

As I previously mentioned, I am an only child and never got the real "skinny" ("Skinny" – expression meaning "the truth") on why my mother could not have more children. Both of my parents come from large families, so it is a bit out of line that I am an only child, but it is what it is. Being born an only child, especially to this family, was the beginning of many "trials and tribulations" that were to last me throughout my entire life until this day. My parents were the source of much, if not all, of my "pain, anger and sorrow" in my life. Though I have always been a "Good Italian Catholic Boy," in time I grew to hate my parents. Many who read this book may not agree with my views about my parents, but I am the one who lived with them – the one who dealt with them on a daily basis; the one who took care of them and gave them both a "good death" in their home, sacrificing so much for the both of them and not to get appreciated from either one of them. Some may argue they sacrificed much for me. Though they clothed, fed and housed me, there was no love in our family. The love I needed, wanted and desired, even to this day, never happened – neither as a child nor an adult. It was just never there, never to be had. This was and is my truth. I make no apologies to anyone as I did the right thing as a son and as a man but the mental, physical, emotional, spiritual, and financial hardships they have put me through are immeasurable and I continue to feel them to this day.

Stupid People

My parents were not just ignorant people they were stupid people. The difference between "Ignorant" and "Stupid" is that you can work with an ignorant person, that is, if they are willing to learn, and they can change and grow from being an ignorant person to becoming an educated person. Conversely a stupid person is ignorant and to top it off think that they "know it all."

As the saying goes "you can't fix stupid!" My mother would fret over pennies being wasted, while hundreds if not thousands of dollars in other areas would be wasted because of her stupidity. In another example, I would spend countless hours trying to teach her how to speak English. She would *yes* me to death about what I would teach, even while correcting her, yet she would go back to speaking her own incorrect English to people. Many times, insulting them, because she did not speak English well to get her point across. Until her death her stupidity cost me in so many ways.

Fighting ... The Other Means of Communication

I grew up in a household where yelling and screaming was the normal method of communication. As the saying goes, there is "yelling and screaming" and then there is "yelling and screaming." The yelling and screaming practiced at my house was most always malicious. Being an "Empath" (Being an **empath** is different from being empathetic. Being empathetic is **when your** heart goes out to someone else, while being an **empath** means **you** can actually feel another person's happiness or sadness in **your** own body) as a child and even now, I have the ability to sense the feeling behind what is being said and not just the words being said. They would be so hurtful to one another which caused me a great amount of emotional pain, distress, and suffering. They would use "words like weapons" against each other, causing a tremendous amount of emotional pain to each other which always ended with my mother crying hysterically. The kind of crying hysterics that "scared the shit out of me" as a young child. When I was younger, I would always be a witness to the "emotional carnage" they did to one another. It hurt me deeply. As I got older, I would go to my room and close the door but the yelling and screaming would still come through the walls and the doors. This affected me tremendously in my younger years and to a lesser extent now that I have become older. However, I do suspect it has triggered some PTSD (Post Traumatic Stress Disorder) within me at times and even now as an adult.

They Did the Best They Could...the Modern-Day Catch Phrase

I have attended many a 12 step meeting, heard many people speak, both mental health professionals and lay people to hear the same classic line: **they did the best they could**. In my family they DID NOT do the best they could. My parents were two selfish people who only cared about themselves. In their minds they fed me, clothed me and housed me, so they performed their responsibilities as parents. They were done with their part as being parents. They come to a strange country not knowing the language, not knowing a single soul, and they chose to isolate themselves socially from other people...and if they do socialize with other people they are constantly being critical of them, constantly being negative and hateful. Both of my parents came from large families, yet they cared less about my emotional needs in being so isolated from others, especially the extended family. Constantly fighting with other extended family members – and as a child not understanding why. All I knew was I was not hanging out with my aunts, uncles and cousins. I never knew or understood where the fighting started within the extended families and whose fault it was. The fighting within my extended family affects me until this day as an adult. I can be with my extended family at an event, usually a funeral, and we feel and act like strangers to one another as there are no bonds of family love between us. It's like being in a room full of unknown people – related by blood only and not true family-love ties. It hurts my heart and spirit tremendously all because my parents were wrapped up in their own "bullshit, drama and egos".

As I got older, I began to dislike my parents more and more to the point of hatred.

Sometimes the Dog is Just the Dog

I don't know what was broken in both of my parents' lives to treat me not like their beloved child and a cherished family member, but more like an animal having its offspring in the wild. I have seen wild animals show more compassion, caring and love to their offspring than my parents showed me, especially my mother. I was to be seen and not heard. I was to obey and not question the reasons why. I was to be the "Good Italian Son." They gave me the basics of life, so I was to be grateful and keep my mouth shut. I remember as a child I could not enjoy the snow falling because that meant my father could not work (being a bricklayer and working outside) and he would be stuck in the house with my mother and the fighting would begin. To this day I don't enjoy a peaceful snowfall…

Someone should have been called…Someone should have come…Someone should have recused me!

I endured a lifetime of yelling and screaming from these two people called my parents. A nightmare that seemed never to end. How can two people who took marriage vows to love and honor each other turn into such miserable people is beyond my scope of understanding. If you're so damn miserable with one another then get a divorce, move on with your respective lives and don't continue to hurt and damage each other and those around you – and in my case, it was just me. I guess "damaged" is the right word as I feel that I am not whole and somewhat "broken." Didn't other extended family members notice or care what was going on in my family and to me? Why didn't other adults in the community notice my parent's behavior? Maybe it was normal for the times. It just caused me a lot of heartache and headache. Though I know every family has its ugly and painful moments, it's not normal when living with "time-bomb parents" not knowing when either one will go off—with or without provocation.

All I know is that I believed someone should have been called.
Someone should have come.
Someone should have rescued me.
No one was called.
No one came.
And no one rescued me.
Ever...

The "Good Italian Son" and Other Fairy Tales

I always have been and continued to be the "Good Italian Son" to the day both of my parents died. Whenever, whatever and whoever my parents needed I was there for them until the last days of their lives. I would handle whatever needed doing so they could both lead comfortable lives and have comfortable deaths. It didn't matter what I did, sacrificed or gave them to make them comfortable as they were both just miserable people. Both were unappreciative of me, all of my efforts and to other people for what was done for them until the day they died. I pray that my reward, for being The Good Italian Son, comes from God as it surely did not come from my parents.

I Should Know...I Should Have Been Taught... I Should Have Been Told

There are so many things in life that I just don't know about as I was never taught or told about. My parents were too busy fighting to learn the American way of life and how to interact with other people. I had to learn about life on my own. Being and living so secluded with my parents, so many things were just never taught or explained to me that most of the time – basically I didn't know what I was doing. As I got older, I learned, as a survival mechanism, to "fake it until I make it" and would study people and did what they did in order to fit in. It was embarrassing for me not to have parents to teach me the basics of socialization. One thing that was called to my attention, several times when I was young, was my being a very "touchy feely" child, not in a bad way but in a way that would invade someone else's personal space. Now, ironically, as an adult, I find people touching me a lot when I interact with them.

I Finally Broke Away... I Thought I Did

The years went by and I learned more emotional survival skills to deal with my parents. Things did not change – they continued to fight like wild dogs, but I learned to deal with it, unfortunately the way I dealt with it was by internalizing all the pain, anger and sorrow. After high school, the Good Italian Son, stayed home, worked so he could take care of his Italian parents and went to the local community college to get his associate degree in Criminal Justice (Police Science). Then the plan was to stay back home and get my Bachelor's degree and then find a job in the Criminal Justice system. Luckily for me things **did not** work out that way. I did graduate with my Associate degree, however, on my way to starting my Bachelor's degree I had a severe anxiety attack and had to be rushed to the hospital. It all caught up to me. The years of pain, anger and sorrow all manifested itself in an uncontrollable anxiety attack. I never had such a thing happen to me. I thought I was going to have a heart attack! I thought I was going to die! I started shaking uncontrollably so my father brought me to the emergency room, they give me a shot of something and eventually my body and mind calmed down. The emergency room doctor advised me to see the hospital psychiatrist. I set up an appointment for the following week to see the psychiatrist, I wrote a 4-page, single-spaced dissertation of what I had been through – and continue to go through – living with my parents. The day of the appointment came and I started talking with the psychiatrist (an old man who would not look me in the eyes: uncaring, imbecile and a complete waste of time and money). He barely looked at the 4-page, single-spaced dissertation I prepared for him and he prescribes me some type of sedative. I'm out the door in less than 10 minutes. The day after I started taking the medication, then it hit me: **I'm not the problem; my parents are the damn problem!** So, I toss the meds and I knew I had to get away from them as my parents were too toxic for me. I decide to go away to school instead of staying home to complete my Bachelor's degree. Now the problem is, it's June and I'm supposed to start classes in late August, where am I going to find an "away college" that will take me on such short notice that has my area of study. I knew that if I stayed home after the anxiety attack episode, sooner than later, the police would be showing up at my parents' home, as I would have killed them both, and I would be leaving in handcuffs. Luckily, through God's grace, I found a state school near Rochester, New York. I called the school, they agreed to interview me, then I jumped on a plane to speak to all the people involved in admittance process and they accepted me to start in August – two months after the anxiety attack. My new life was about to begin away from my parents! I finally broke away! I thought I did! And I was wrong! The "Good Italian Son Syndrome" is more complex and complicated than it may first appear. I spoke with my Aunt Theresa (the only person in this world who ever showed me any type of love), who I loved dearly, yet another "Screamer" just like my father (as she was my father's sister). I called, telling her that I was going away to college and she said the words that burn in my mind to this day, "Don't abandon your Mother." That's it. The "Secret Weapon" of the "Italian Mother Guilt" kicks in. Comparable in the Jewish culture of "Jewish Mother Guilt," the "Italian Son Guilt" is just as powerful against the Good Italian Son as the "Jewish Mother Guilt" is against the "Nice Jewish Boy." Think of it as the "Kryptonite" rendering the Good Italian Son powerless! So, when I thought I had broken away from my parents – that was not the case. In the words of Al Pacino from the Godfather III movie, "Just when I thought I was out ... they pull me back in."

You Broke my Heart Freddo, You Broke my Heart...Family Betrayal

I watched the Godfather II (yes I'm a big fan, being Italian and all) about a year or so after it came out and I was shocked to see a scene (it was tastefully done, but shocking nonetheless, where you don't see the actual shooting but by hearing it instead you

<u>definitely know</u> what happens) where Al Pacino (who now has become the Godfather) has his older brother Freddo (Alfredo) killed. It's more of an execution than an assassination, regardless dead is dead. Initially when I first watched and mentally processed the scene, I was shocked! How can a family member kill another family member! How can a brother kill another brother! How can a Catholic person kill another from the same faith no less!

The Godfather movies are usually played several times a year in Godfather marathons, so over the years I have viewed all the Godfather movies several times. Because of all the pain, anger and sorrow my parents caused me, the above scene is making more and more sense to me. The emotional pain of family betrayal, especially from parents who are your "Creators" is so raw, so hurtful and so unimaginable, that an act just as raw, hurtful and unimaginable is needed to remedy the pain to the Soul.

I thought of murdering my parents several times and not in a way that just lives in one's mind but in a real way; however, through God's grace, once again, I did not go through with the act of murder. I knew I would feel good for a few moments then my world would start crumbling around me. My guilty conscience and Catholic faith would catch up to me. My personal beliefs about what happens when people crossover by murder (They roam the earth until their souls are avenged, as well as the whole Karma thing), and then the authorities would catch up to me, sooner rather than later. I've watched too many crime drama shows to know that I would be viewed by the police as their prime suspect, since I had the most to gain by my parents' death and being an only child and all.

My parents gave me a "house" to live in, but they didn't give what I needed, wanted and desired: a "home" based on love, support and emotional safety. It made and continues to make so many things in my life so very difficult at times. I did what I had to do to survive emotionally within that setting. I'm not proud of some of the things I have done in my life, but the pain, anger and sorrow got so bad at times that I did what I had to do to feel better and stop the emotional pain. It never ceases to surprise me how so many people lack the empathy to understand this. They had it and have it good in so many ways, so they think all the world has it the same way. Wake up! The rest of the world didn't and doesn't have it as good as you, so try, just once, to be a little more compassionate to others. Walk a moment in their lives. You just might become a better human being for it!

I did the following exercise about a half dozen times over the years and continue to do it when things "bubble up" regarding my parents:

EXERCISE 01: BEING MAD AT MY PARENTS - TELL <u>EACH</u> PARENT (and/or CAREGIVER) WHY YOU ARE MAD AT THEM AND GIVE REASON(S) WHY YOU ARE MAD AT THEM. Take a piece of paper(s) and tell <u>each</u> Parent (and/or Caregiver) the reason(s) why you are mad at them. When you're done. Go outside, in a safe place, in a fireproof container and take your letter to them and burn it. The purpose of the exercise is to get the "mad" out of you and place it into the paper and then burn the paper, so the "mad" feelings are out of your system (psyche) and sent into the air so they don't come back to bother you any longer. Do this exercise as many times as necessary (Does not have to be in one sitting, but can be over a period of time) until all of the "mad" is out of you. Fire is a very important basic element, that helps to transmute (change in form, nature or substance) things. Fire needs to be respected when working with it. Remember to always be safe when working with fire.

PART II

THE FEELING'S AND EMOTIONS

CHAPTER 2

God, Where the Hell Were You!

When I am speaking about God, I try not to use either the masculine or the feminine as I believe that God is neither and both at the same time. Furthermore, I believe God is in all of us specifically in what I believe to be the "Soul." It is my belief that we as human being are made up of four (4) unique components, these are: The Physical (the Body), The Mental (the Mind), The Emotional (The Heart – emotional feelings, the emotional heart) and The Spirit (the Life Force within all of humans). I further believe the Soul is the direct interface with God. While we can try to run away from God, I believe God is "hardwired" into all of us and in our being. God has given all of us the gift of "Free Will" to either acknowledge the God presence within each of us, ignore it, or pretend it's not there. As our parent's DNA is in us as their children so I believe a piece of "God's Soul" is in each and everyone one of us, as we are God's children. I believe the Spirit is not the Soul. The Spirit is the life force which animates the human body that is within us all. Furthermore, I believe that once we die the Spirit leaves the body with the Soul, the Soul reunites with God and our Spirit based on its mission (learning), will either reincarnate again (with the Soul) if it needs to learn more to complete its mission, or will stop reincarnating once it has completed its mission (learning) and help the living with their mission (learning) while on the other side.

Though I am a Minister (and technically work directly for God), that doesn't mean I don't get mad at God! The kind of mad I get at God is sometimes "One Fisted" type of mad, but occasionally it's the "Two Fisted" kind. This is where I yell and either shake one or two fists at God depending on how mad I am, and what specific reason I am mad at God.

One would think that because I work for God and have an "in" with God, so to speak, being an employee and all, that life would be going my way but <u>NOOOOOO</u>! I have been and continue to experience my share of trials and tribulations. As I have mentioned previously my parents caused me great distress which I still deal with to this day as an adult. **<u>What if</u>** my upbringing was different? **<u>What if</u>** I had loving parents, I had brothers and sisters, I had a caring extended family? **<u>What if</u>** I had chosen a different career path? Gotten married? Had kids? The "What ifs" are always haunting me. I grieve for a life I never had.

The one thing I do know is how easily it could have been for me with all my pain, anger and sorrow to have become an alcoholic, drug addict, a criminal, or done other bad things to myself and others. It is only through God's grace that these things did not happen to me (or worse) that I would have taken my own life.

If you need to get mad at God, you go right ahead. God won't hate you; you won't be struck by lightning, sent into any type of hell, or damnation and the world won't come to an end if you do get mad at God. God gave us the gift of free will and with that gift comes the ability to get mad at God from time to time. God can take it!

EXERCISE 02: BEING MAD AT GOD (THAT IS IF YOU ARE MAD AT GOD) TELL GOD YOU ARE MAD AT GOD AND GIVE THE REASON(S) WHY YOU ARE MAD AT GOD. Take a piece of paper(s) and tell God the reason(s) why you are mad at God. Yes, this exercise is the same as the one in Chapter 1 but this one is about being mad at God. When you're done, go outside, in a safe place, in a fireproof container and take your letter to God and burn it. The purpose of the exercise is to get the "mad" out of you and place it into the paper and then burn the paper, so the "mad" reasons are out of your system (psyche) and sent into the air so they don't come back to bother you any longer. Fire is a very important basic element, that helps to transmute (change in form, nature or substance) things and needs to be respected when working with it. Remember always be safe when working with fire.

CHAPTER 3

Your Feelings Will Wait...

I'm a big admirer of Oprah Winfrey (Creator of the OWN Network, Television Personality and Author). I have been watching her and continue to watch her on television since she went national with her television show and I still like the way she was, and still is, a seeker of knowledge about the human condition and helping all of us with the same. She would probe things on a national stage that others did not, and she would ask the tough questions about the most personal of things that most people have gone through. She would, in time, comment on the trials and tribulations of her own life and how it affected her. On one of her shows, she said something very profound many years ago that stuck with me and rings true even to this day. She said, "Your feelings will wait." At the time I really did not know what those words meant but as I got older those words really resonated within me. Truth be told that is exactly what happened to me. What her expression "Your feelings will wait" came to mean to me was when your life finally calms down, and it will one day, all the suppressed, repressed and painful feelings will start to "bubble up" and will have to be acknowledged and dealt with if you want to move forward with your life.

You Have to Put in "The Work"

There are some things in life you can go around, go under and even go over but the really important things in life you have to go through them. There are no shortcuts. No one can go through them for you. You must do it yourself. You must put in "The

Work". I have put in the work for my life and continue to put in the work for my pain, anger and sorrow. I'm still doing the work, though not as often, deep and profound as when I first started my personal journey but there is always something bubbling up from time to time to be dealt with. Many people ask how long does this "work" take to be completed? The short answer is it depends on what you have been through, how it affects and continues to affect you? The long answer is it's going to "take what it takes." What's the reward for all of this "work"? Your reward is you releasing all of that pain, anger and sorrow – being content and happy, seeing life through a different set of eyes maybe for the very first time. God says, "You're worth it." Most of all, you owe to yourself to be the best person you can be. There is light at the end of the tunnel, you just have to put in the work to get there. Put in the "work," you're worth it!

EXERCISE 03: JOURNALING - BUY YOURSELF A NOTEBOOK WITH LINED PAPER AND START WRITING DOWN WHATEVER COMES UP.

Start getting into the habit of writing and you will be surprised what "bubbles up." You will start seeing in your writings what you need to deal with that has been suppressed, repressed, including any painful feelings. These feelings, emotions, events, etc. is the "work" that you have to do, process, and heal yourself from. There are professionals to help you with the work (your work), self-help groups, and books but ultimately you still must do the work yourself. You don't have to do it alone. There are some resources in the back of this book to give you some suggestions.

CHAPTER 4

Pain is Pain, Just the Wrapper is Different

What I've learned over the years about people's emotional pain (including my own) is that "Pain is Pain" and the "Wrapper" (the outside symptom of the emotional pain) may look different. The "Pain" here is the emotional pain as to why we are hurting inside, in our Spirit. The "Wrapper" is the outside manifestation of our "Pain," be it drug/alcohol addiction, overeating, sexual behavior, out of control gambling, spending, etc. Though whatever the cause of our pain, the main issue here is: we "hurt" on the inside, we hurt emotionally, we hurt where it cannot be seen by other people and can only be experienced by those of us that hurt and experienced by our Spirit. What may be perceived as a trivial experience to one person may be devasting to another person. Emotions are not logical or linear, we feel what we feel regardless of what other people's perception about the situation is. One person may go to war and see and experience human atrocities and not be affected, while another person is never the same again and is emotionally in pain. I have observed that some people who are perceived to have "everything" (good career, fame, fortune, good health, family, etc.) are miserable. Of course, there are those people who have everything and are happy, grateful and help others as well. Conversely I have seen people who have "nothing" and are happy, grateful and help others with what they have.

Personally, over the years I have just been treating the "symptoms" of my emotional pain. My "treatments" of choice were food, sex and alcohol. When I was younger these "treatments" would last for a while but as I have gotten older the effectiveness of these "treatments" have become less and less effective. It has gotten to the point where the "treatments" rarely last more than a half-hour or so after their administration. I can't fill the "holes in my soul" with my "treatments" any longer because it is detrimental to my health and wellbeing. It's like putting liquid in a funnel. For a brief moment, the funnel's full and "all is good" then within a very short time the funnel goes empty. Fill it up again and the same thing happens, it goes empty. Again, and again and again. The funnel goes empty. You get the picture.

What to do, I asked myself? It was time to get to the "cause of my pain." It was time to heal the "holes in my soul" once and for all. I have been on my healing journey for well over 35 years, working with all type of medical, psychological, and spiritual professionals. Some have helped me and some not so much. What I have learned and what has helped me the most is dealing with my emotional pain directly, working "through the pain." I have "put in the work" and continue to "put in work" on myself and the work continues to evolve as I continue to evolve, heal and grow. Sometimes the work has been painful, sometimes the work has been hard, but I can tell you one thing every time I do "put in work" I do feel better. The more work I put in, the better I feel. I ask (God) when will I be finished with my work and the answer (that comes back) is: "It will be over when it's over." In the meantime, life isn't so bad and has gotten better. My emotional pain is like a bad back for me. If I take care of my back by eating right, exercising and staying calm by handling my stress…it's a manageable situation. If I don't take care of my back, then my back goes out, and I am in pain walking around like the hunchback of Notre Dame!

If I do my work on me, dealing with whatever comes up from my soul and I support it with prayer, meditation, connecting with nature, eating right and being of service to others, the suicidal thoughts don't come to me as often as they used to. And even if they do come they tend not to bother me as much, last as long and tend to go away fairly quickly.

EXERCISE 04: IDENTIFYING YOUR EMOTIONAL PAIN

In your notebook start to write down all of your "Emotional Pain." This is your personal notebook, and nobody needs to see it. Go to a quiet place and center yourself. Prayer and meditation is very helpful. Being in nature is also very helpful. Write the emotional pain that you carry so it can be processed and released from your soul. Start getting into the habit of writing and you will be surprised what "bubbles up." You will start seeing in your writings what you need to deal with that has been suppressed and repressed, including any painful feelings. These feelings, emotions, events, etc. is the "work" that you have to do, to process and heal yourself. There are professionals to help you with the work (your work), self-help groups and books, but ultimately you still must do the work yourself. You don't have to do it alone. There are resources towards the end of the book to give you some suggestions.

CHAPTER 5

Loneliness, Lonely, Alone…

For me loneliness is something I have had to deal with my entire life. In my childhood it was thrust upon me due to my parent's way of living and behavior. I have a large extended family and we are not close, so they are more like strangers than relatives. When I go to major family events (meaning funerals) there is no sense of family love. Kisses on the cheek from relatives are empty gestures with no love behind them. It pains me deeply that there is not a true "family love connection." Since we did not grow up together in love there is no love now. Neither do I get a feeling that loving relationships can be established so I don't bother to put the time or the energy into them. The few relatives I do talk to tend to be empty conversations at best. I am invited over more out of a sense of pity than love. And if I do go over I tend to be the "odd person out" and don't fit in for a host of different reasons (I'm not married and don't have children, my political views are different, my hair is long, etc.) The experience is more of a "headache and heartache" than that of a supportive extended family gathering. So, I have just resigned myself of having an extended family in theory but not in practice.

Though I had and have friends, it's just not the same as having brothers and sisters growing up who are going through life with you and sharing similar life experiences. I mean with siblings you can discuss major life events, changes and challenges with, to the minor things like what clothes look best on me. Call anytime. Share a meal together. Hang out on the holidays. Just so many activities that just never have or will happen. It would have been nice to be an uncle and have a few nieces and nephews to spoil rotten and get yelled at by their parents, but it just was not meant to be for me.

I have spent and continue to spend about 80% of my life alone. Some of that time by destiny's hand and some by my own hand. This is my normal. Ironically, I rarely feel lonely and when I do feel lonely I put a few dollars in my pocket, go out to a pub-type restaurant and I meet people, more often than not. I have no problem meeting new people. Sometimes the new people I meet become acquaintances. I have plenty of "acquaintances" but very few close friends and that's fine with me. Acquaintances come and go but friends last. Sometimes I spend time in nature, go to a church, a library and other places where there are people and then I don't feel lonely anymore.

Now being alone is a completely different matter for me. For the longest time in my life, really until recently, I felt alone in life. Not connected to anyone or anything. That has been and at times continues to be very emotionally painful for me. Not being a part of something, like a family, a group, a tribe - something, anything, where I belong, where I fit in, where I am welcomed. I have at times (many times), as many have said before me, "been in a crowded room and felt completely alone." It's something I have worked on and continue to work on (not feeling completely alone). Tools like prayer and meditation, my spiritual beliefs of guardian angels and spirit guides. Working with spiritual teachers that have explained to me we are never really alone – maybe, sometimes, we may feel that way on this physical plain, but on the spiritual plain our guides, guardians, and ancestors are always with us. Though at times I forget my own personal experience with God, I am reminded by other people's stories which give me hope and comfort that makes my "aloneness" bearable. Now I feel that I have a better understanding and more control of my aloneness, so it is not as frightening and emotionally painful as it once was to me.

EXERCISE 05: BEING ALONE – GET INVOLVED WITH SOMETHING MEANINGFUL.

We don't need to be alone if we do not choose to. Get involve with something meaningful in your life. Be it a local food pantry, animal rescue, or whatever resonates with you. You will find that by helping others that need help, you will no longer be alone...by meeting new people and having new life experiences. By helping others, we are always helping ourselves. A good place to start is online by going to websites like www.MeetUp.com, Facebook (and other social media websites), or to your favorite search engine and typing the words "Local Groups Near Me."

CHAPTER 6

I'm Less Than...

For the longest time in my life, I felt that I was "less than." I suspect it was due to my upbringing and all the pain, anger and sorrow I suffered, and to a lesser extent, continue to suffer. I felt as though if my parents did not treat me with any type of "high self-esteem" so then I must not be worthy of the same. There must be something wrong with me, I must be less than good, less than worthy, less than deserving. I must be "less than." Though I'm a grown man and intellectually know better, my self esteem still suffers. I am not as confident as I should be. Though I portray myself as strong at times, many a time I am just as unsure of myself as well. It's a day-to-day thing: a day-to-day battle. Am I going to be strong and confident today and face my fears, my pain, anger and sorrow and do what I have to do today, or find excuses and do the opposite? It's taken me a long time to address, mend and still I am continually healing my "core wounds." It's an inside job. I would like to have someone just heal me, but unfortunately it's just not happening that way. I'm good for a little while then something else "bubbles up" that I have to deal with, luckily I have the tools and the people to help me deal and heal from what comes bubbling up. I keep on asking the question, "when will the healing be completed?" And the answer I keep on getting is "it will be over when it's over." The healing practitioners tell me, that due to the type of healing being done it has to assimilate into your spiritual being. I have noticed that to be true. Unfortunately, that doesn't make me feel any better as being patient is not one of my virtues. However, I must say that GOD has always pulled my ass out of the fire on more than one occasion and when things get/are bad - more often than not and sooner rather than later – help comes my way in so many different forms. Though I am an All-Faiths Minister myself and work for GOD I am not immune from the trials and tribulations of life as I previously mentioned. It appears that "I have to learn what I teach" and have to "talk the talk" and "walk the walk" myself.

As an All-Faith Minister I believe there are many Paths to GOD. I created the graphic below to demonstrate the concept to people:

© Copyright. www.GodLovesYouAndMe.org

Though I am born a Catholic and will die a Catholic, but in between not so much. I have studied most if not all the major religions and spiritual traditions including some that are not as well-known as others, but one thing I have observed is that each practice has value in bringing people closer to God, in healing people, and is a contributor to the wellbeing of humanity. It is as though GOD, in his/her infinite wisdom, did not give any one religion or spiritual practice all the answers and all the keys, with the knowledge being there for humanity to experience so there are multiple ways to get to GOD. Find your spiritual path from the above graphic or create your own personal path to GOD. I did, you can too. Though I was raised Catholic I work with Shamans. When I go to church I feel connected to GOD in one way and when I work with the Mother Earth, nature and the Shamans I feel connected to GOD in another way. When I work with people I see GOD work and feel GOD is with us and helping us. Either way I'm connecting with and to GOD.

Find your path to GOD. Where to start? Nature is a good place. Go and sit in a park. Pray, meditate, and/or just be still. Things will come to you. The internet has wonderful sources of knowledge about all the various spiritual traditions and is constantly growing. YouTube has almost an infinite number of guided meditations on any spiritual subject you would like to explore. Use a search engine and learn about religions and the various spiritual traditions of the world. Go to a church, synagogue, or a mosque. Spend time and/or volunteer at a "New Age" (there's really nothing New Age about it as some of the things you'll learn have been around for hundreds if not thousands of years 😊)" store. As the opportunities of learning, growing, and healing are endless I encourage you to start and/or continue your journey to find GOD, to find yourself. It is said in The Holy Bible: "I and the Father are ONE (John 10:30)."

EXERCISE 06: THIS IS A TWO-PART EXERCISE. PART ONE: HAVE YOU EVER FELT LESS THAN? IF SO, DESCRIBE IN DETAIL IN YOUR NOTEBOOK WHAT YOU FEEL. DO PART ONE OVER AND OVER AGAIN UNTIL YOU CANNOT WRITE ANY MORE. PART TWO: FIND YOUR SPIRITUAL PATH OR CREATE YOUR OWN PERSONAL PATH TO GOD. READ BOOKS, ATTEND RELIGIOUS AND SPIRITUAL SERVICES. FIND THE PATH THAT IS RIGHT FOR YOU. Write about it in your notebook. Document what you learn, where you go, who you meet, etc.

CHAPTER 7

Pain, Anger and Sorrow

I have mentioned my pain, anger and sorrow many times in this book. These things reflect my own personal struggles which I have had to endure my entire life. I am always asking the question WHY? Specifically, WHY ME? The answer I have been given by some very intelligent, spiritual and loving beings is WHY NOT YOU? Who these beings are is not important, it's the answers that struck me to be important. Why not me? I initially was shocked to hear these words, as it took me many years to understand them and their meaning. Why not me? Who am I to be exempted from the pain, anger and sorrow that life gives to human beings?

As the years passed by, I slowly started to understand that maybe, just maybe, there is a meaning in all of the pain, anger and sorrow that I have experienced. Maybe there are lessons to be learned from all of my negative experiences. That unfortunately, there are some lessons that one must experience themselves, firsthand, to really get their meanings – no second account, no other people's experiences, no "I read about it." You just have to go through the fire yourself and live the full effect of the fire and come out the other side and live to tell about it. I believe that must be the case for me. All my pain, anger and sorrow should have caused me to take my own life but it hasn't and while I still do have an occasional bad day and I still think of killing myself it pales in comparison to the days when I actually thought about doing it executing the plan to the smallest detail. When I was in the throes of suicidal depression I would enter a dark void that seemed, in my mind, to never end. What I learned over the years is that what a person thinks about themselves is a matter of personal perspective. One person's misery is another person's joy. Is my life better or worse than someone else's life? Maybe on the physical plane, pain at face value might be the case but even then we all know people that "appear to have it all" and are miserable and people that "have nothing" but are happy.

What I learned is: My Happiness is MY Responsibility. That may sound nice to say but it did me no good when I was miserable on the inside. This simple but profound concept taught me that my own happiness is an "inside job" and that if I wanted to be happy I would have to work on it myself. That enlightened thought of "my happiness is my responsibility" just "sucks ass" and did very little to easy my pain, anger and sorrow at the time it came to me. HOWEVER, as I did and continue to work on myself, and did some painful work at that, I started feeling better about myself. It's as though with each exercise I did, I released just a little more of the pain, anger and sorrow until one day I know it will be completely gone and be filled with love, happiness and joy. I don't like the fact that no one can do the work but me. I don't like the fact that sometimes painful things come out that need to be dealt with. I do like the way I feel after the work is done and things have settled down. Sometimes, and it's happening more and more often, when I do more work, I realize I actually have a pretty good life. It like going to the gym and eating right, I do not like doing either but when I do, I feel better for it and I'm glad I did it. That's my next challenge, *my weight*, but that's a topic for another book ☺.

EXERCISE 07: THIS IS A TWO-PART EXERCISE. <u>**PART ONE:**</u> DO YOU HAVE PAIN, ANGER AND SORROW IN YOUR LIFE? IF SO, DESCRIBE IN DETAIL IN YOUR NOTEBOOK WHAT YOU FEEL. DO PART ONE OVER AND OVER AGAIN UNTIL YOU CANNOT WRITE ANY MORE ABOUT THE TOPIC MENTIONED. <u>**PART TWO:**</u> WHAT CAN YOU DO TO HELP YOU BE HAPPY?

CHAPTER 8

I Have Seen the Darkness – Many, Many Times...

Many people speak about the "dark night of the soul," how their lives have hit bottom and their lives have changed. I have had so many "dark nights of the soul" I thought I was living in some parts of Alaska where they don't see the sun about 67 days. Though I may be somewhat joking about that, here's the truth about entering "the darkness," "my darkness" is not at all, even the slightest bit amusing. I have experienced darkness that has been nothing short of terrifying. I have entered parts of my mind that should not have been experienced by anyone alone. I have encountered a darkness that seemed like a bottomless pit of misery that when going through it made me feel that there was no hope...no future...no light. I have experienced a terror that occasionally haunts me until this day. When I experienced this "darkness" suicide seemed like a logical relief from "the pain" of the darkness. I don't have anything profound to say as to how I got through my darkness other than I must believe it was my faith, my belief in God (Psalm 40:2 He brought me up also out of an horrible pit, out of the miry clay, and set my feet upon a rock, and established my goings). Because there were times I wanted to jump into the endless abyss, thinking it would end my emotional pain. I wanted all the pain to end, once and for all. I wanted to be set free. Being an Inter-Faith Minister, all the teaching and instruction has taught me many things. While some things cannot be proven until death but for me there are just way too many coincidences among various religious teachings about certain things (like Karma for example, in Hinduism and Buddhism, the sum of a person's actions in this and previous states of existence, viewed as deciding their fate in future existences) for these teachings not to be true in my mind. There are spiritual consequences about taking your own life that need to be at least read about, acknowledged and understood (there will be an upcoming chapter about the Spiritual Consequences of Suicide). We must be aware of the responsibilities we have to every single person whose life we have touched and would have touched in a very significant way by each one of us. Should these obligations not be met there will be spiritual consequences that will need to be addressed. Whether you live and believe a certain religious practice (example, Suicide is a Sin if you are Catholic), or follow no religious or spiritual practice, none of us can accurately predict the future. What might have been a reason to commit suicide turns out to be only a rough patch in one's life necessary to go through to achieve a greater happiness than was thought possible.

I know emotions are not logical or linear. One feels what one feels and the emotional pain of being suicidal and of suicide thoughts can be unbearable at times but there is help (remember the number in the front of this book for the Suicidal Hotline – there is no shame in calling it when you need help or someone to talk to), there is hope even in the darkest of times.

Here is a prayer (more prayers in the back of the book) if you have suicidal thoughts:

Lord, I come before You with a heavy heart. I feel so much and yet sometimes I feel nothing at all. I don't know where to turn,

who to talk to, or how to deal with the things going on in my life. You see everything, Lord. You know everything, Lord. Yet when I seek you it is so hard to feel You here with me. Lord, help me through this. I don't see any other way to get out of this. There is no light at the end of my tunnel, yet everyone says You can show it to me. Lord, help me find that light. Let it be Your light. Give me someone to help. Let me feel You with me. Lord, let me see what You provide and see an alternative to taking my life. Let me feel Your blessings and comfort. Amen.

Never give up hope. God can find a way where there appears to be no way. God can see things that we cannot and make things happen in ways we may not understand. Meet God halfway by praying, meditating and being patient and good things will happen, sooner than later. Give God a chance to work in your life. It has happened for me and it will happen for you!

EXERCISE 08: HAVE YOU EXPERIENCED 'THE DARKNESS' IN YOUR LIFE? IF SO, DESCRIBE IT IN DETAIL AND WRITE ABOUT IT OVER AND OVER AGAIN UNTIL YOU CANNOT WRITE ANY MORE ABOUT IT.

CHAPTER 9

Depression

I think I have been depressed the major part of my life and not the kind of depression that's like rainy days and Mondays that always get me down. I mean the type of depression that is clinical and genetic. I suspect I get it from my mother as she had a "boat load" of psychological "dis-eases of the mind and emotions." Being she was an illiterate immigrant with the education of a first grader and obstinate as the day is long, she would never admit she had any type of issue or problem and it was always "other people" that made her behave in the manor she did. Also being working-class immigrants they did not have the luxury of having mental health issues, working with psychologists, and taking anti-depression medications.

Regardless where it came from, I suffer from and deal with the "Big D" – Depression. Only having worked on myself and continuing to work on myself have I come to this conclusion. I have been "asymptomatic" (Asymptomatic - In medicine, a disease is considered asymptomatic if a patient is a carrier for a disease or infection but experiences no symptoms. A condition might be asymptomatic if it fails to show the noticeable symptoms with which it is usually associated). Usually my depression lies dormant until the events of life trigger it. Taking care of my parents for over 18 years put me in a major depression. Having to put my professional and personal life on hold to take care of them, losing tremendous amounts of money by rarely working to taking care of them and their medical, legal and personal affairs, gaining over

50 pounds and my health (both mental and emotional) suffering as well.

I have noticed over the years that my major depression has been linked to my life events. As my life events would change and get better so would my depression lift as well. This was evident to me when I had my incident with my anxiety attack and having been rushed to the hospital. Once I made the decision to go away to school and leave the toxic environment of my parents' home my depression started to lift and leave me. This was one thing that has gone into "remission" (the term *remission* is often used in speaking of sufferers from cancers whose symptoms lessen or disappear. In such a case, the disease is said to be "in remission." The period of remission may last only briefly or may extend over several months or years), but still shows itself whenever my thoughts of suicide arise.

Though my thoughts of suicide are not as bad as they once were and don't last as long as they do, they are still in my mind, somewhere, nonetheless. I view my suicidal thoughts and my "mental cancer" that occasionally bothers me as "asymptomatic" and is currently in "remission." Keeping myself well is important; physically, mentally, emotionally and spiritually. Physically by watching what I eat, I have noticed how food affects my mood and energy level. Mentally by watching what I feed my mind. Not watching a lot of violence, not listening to negative and hateful people and reading positive, uplifting and helpful materials. Our minds work like computers – you put garbage in, and you get garbage out. Emotionally by being more compassionate and helpful to others and being more compassionate to myself (that's a tough one for me to learn and do). Spiritually by spending time in nature, praying, meditating, and asking God for help. I notice that if I do the above I'm okay and don't have suicidal thoughts. I also noticed that if I stray away from the above my life starts getting uneasy and my thoughts start going to that bad place in my mind, etc.

If you're depressed or even feel that you have been in a "funk" for more than a few weeks reach out and talk to someone about it. It may be just a small valley in your life, or it may be the start of something not so good, especially if it's happening more often than not. The world has changed and continues to change, there is nothing to be ashamed about. We all need help in our lives one time or the other, including me. Though I work for God directly (as a Minister) that doesn't exempt me from the trials and tribulations of being human as I have mentioned. Believe me I have asked God to spare me all the pain, anger and sorrow I have experienced and continue to experience in my life – and you know what God told me – God loves me too much and he loves all of his/her children the same and it's all part of learning and growing, so we can be strong and help ourselves and help other people.

EXERCISE 09: HAVE YOU EVER BEEN DEPRESSED OR ARE DEPRESSED NOW? IF SO, DESCRIBE IT IN DETAIL AND WRITE ABOUT IT OVER AND OVER AGAIN UNTIL YOU CANNOT WRITE ANY MORE ABOUT IT.

CHAPTER 10

Shame

I started experiencing shame at a young age and once again the main cause that I could identify was my parents. Being immigrants, not speaking English well and for the most part keeping to themselves did not really bother me. What did bother me was the way they behaved in public. Yelling and screaming at each other like wild animals. It did not matter where we were, or what the situation was, or who was there, if an argument broke out you can rest assured yelling and screaming was not too far behind. Because my parents did not have mastery of the English language they would say things that made sense to them but you hard pressed to figure out what they meant. What comes to mind when I was about 10 years old and there was a problem with the utility bill. My father had me call the utility company and see what the problem was with the bill. While the representative was explaining to me about the issue with bill and I'm trying to understand her, my father is yelling/screaming at me in the background to tell them exactly what he wants said. Tell them "you foolish me" and "it no true!" None of this making any sense except to my father.

Besides it not being good English, the phrases simply don't make any sense. So, with one ear I'm listening to him and the other ear I'm listening to the utilities representative and I'm stressing (and I mean big time), yelling at my father so I can get a resolution about the utility bill and just feeling ashamed that I'm being put through all this.

Another time my mother brought me to school for a conference with my third-grade teacher. My teacher was explaining to my mother the issues I was having at school at the time, which she barely understood. She says to the teacher, "If Oreste no do good in school, my husband kick him!" What she meant to deliver is, "If Oreste does not well in school my husband will punish him." Luckily, this was a time before Child Protective Services, which was not as prevalent then as it is today, and the teacher did not escalate the issue to the authorities for who knows what might have happened to me.

Though I always had love for my parents growing up, they both just didn't "give a damn" when, where and how they shamed me. For this reason, I rarely brought friends home to meet my parents. As I got older and started making friends, some of which were girls, who would call me at home, my mother told me it was inappropriate for girls to call me at home. So, the minute I could make money, which was at the age of 13, I put a separate telephone line in my bedroom ending that nonsense.

The shame I carried about my parents throughout my entire life continues to be with me and is something I continue to work on. I work on separating the shame from who I am. My parents were my parents for their own reasons, and I am who I am – we're just different. I was not ASHAMED of my parents for who they were, they made me feel SHAME for their behaviors not caring how their behaviors would impact me, my life and growing up alone. I try to think about my parents as individuals and understand what they went through in their lives but all the pain, anger and sorrow they caused me makes it difficult for me to be compassionate towards them. I grieve a family life I never had. What if they were loving, supportive, and caring parents? What if I had a loving, caring and supportive extended family? Who would I have become? Where would I be now? What if I ask myself so many times? What if...

EXERCISE 10: HAVE YOU EVER FELT SHAME? IF SO, DESCRIBE IT IN DETAIL AND WRITE ABOUT IT OVER AND OVER AGAIN UNTIL YOU CANNOT WRITE ANY MORE ABOUT IT.

CHAPTER 11

Rage!!!

I went through a lot of rage in my life. Bouts of inexplicable rage that would come out of nowhere. As time went by I would ask the question why? When I would have spells of calmness, I started to investigate rage so I could get a better understanding of what rage was and what I could do about it. Rage, defined by the Merriam-Webster Dictionary, is "violent and uncontrolled anger." In my research on rage I learned it is the leading cause of anger is a person's environment. Stress, financial issues, abuse, poor social or familial situations, and overwhelming requirements on your time and energy can all contribute to the formation of anger. It all started to make sense and have a root cause.

I was truly a "Rage-o-holic" and like an alcoholic I needed my fix of rage ever so often to feel good about myself, no matter the cost to myself or those around me. I would explode with rage at a minor provocation for it was just an excuse to release the "pressure cooker" of my anger.

As I got older I became and still am a believer that a person can help themselves (sometimes with the help of others but usually the work they do is on themselves and no one can do it but the individual person) once they know the root cause of the problem, have the right tools to do the job, and know how to use them. I always want to get to the root of a problem because fixing symptoms usually doesn't last very long and/or another symptom usually pops up to takes its place. So, I started reading books on healing rage. In the meantime, my rage was getting out of control. I could no longer "box in" my rage. I couldn't control it anymore. My professional life was on the rocks and my personal life was not much better. The more books I read and more exercises I did the better I was feeling, and my rage quieted down a lot as I was understanding the cause of my rage and releasing all that was associated with all that anger. I have listed some books on rage in the Resources Section in back of the book that you may find helpful if rage is an issue in your life.

I rarely rage now but still wonder if it is tied into my long-term thoughts of suicide and if rage is a symptom of that mental/emotional "dis-ease."

EXERCISE 11: HAVE YOU EVER EXPERIENCED RAGE? DO YOU CONTINUE TO EXPERIENCE RAGE? IF SO, DESCRIBE IT IN DETAIL AND WRITE ABOUT IT OVER AND OVER AGAIN UNTIL YOU CANNOT WRITE ANY MORE ABOUT IT.

CHAPTER 12

Addiction – My Crutch to Never Healing

I never thought of myself as being addicted to anything but as I got older I saw that not to be true. I thought I was stronger than that as I never needed anything or anybody to survive. Then I found out that that's not true for me as well. My addictions have changed over the years but there are there nonetheless. When I was younger I was addicted to food, sex, and alcohol and not necessarily in that order and to various degrees for each addiction. Also, as I got older, the depth, breathe and scope of each addition changed. What would satiate (satisfy me, make me content, fill me) me when I was younger did not satiate me as I got older and/or the feelings of satiety didn't last as long as well. When I was younger I would drink my fill and I would be content with myself for a while, usually a week or so, and as I got older I would drink my fill and the feelings of being content would last less and less to the point that within a half hour of drinking I would be my unhappy self again. This would happen with my other additions as well. I knew at that point that whatever I threw into the "Holes in my Soul" would not FILL the "Holes in my Soul" and would neither make me feel whole and complete.

It was a wake-up call for me and to stop fooling myself by not treating the symptoms and get to the root cause of the issues in my life. I started working on myself with exercises mentioned in this book, I worked with other people that helped me tremendously as well, and last but not the least, my faith and belief in God (using prayer and meditation). As I mentioned previously, for me in this lifetime, the issues have been with my parents and all that come with being raised by them, living with them, and caring for them until their deaths. I had to put in the work and process all the emotional pain, anger and sorrow they put me through. There's no point to discuss how long it took to process it all, it took what it took, and I feel much better for it now. Am I 100% healed/cured? Probably not. I still have "pangs" of emotional pain, anger and sorrow of all that they put me through, but I don't go to that dark place in my mind and heart anymore and that is a very good thing for me.

I used my addictions as my "crutches." I would lean on my addictions when I was in emotional pain. I came close to breaking my crutches a few times by indulging a bit too much on my addictions, but luckily I was able to pull myself back to reality before I went overboard or crossed over the line of no return. I still use my crutches on occasion, when I have a bad day, but not as much as I used to as they don't give me the "pick me up" lift and support they once did. And that's okay too as it's telling me I'm stronger and getting stronger, so I don't need my crutches as much anymore because they really aren't doing much for me anyway.

EXERCISE 12: DO YOU THINK YOU HAVE ADDICTION(S)? IF SO, WRITE ABOUT THEM IN DETAIL.

CHAPTER 13

I Fooled the World but was Only Fooling Myself...

I went through most of my life with the outward appearance that everything was "just fine" in my life and I was rough and tumble like an "alligator bag" (Besides being a fashion accessory, "alligator bags" are reliable plastic food storage bags that make it easy to store all types of foods. Can be found in your supermarket 😊). In my twisted, warped and ego-centric mind, I thought I was fooling the world with my "outward" appearance of my life, while on the inside I was miserable, sad and alone. I wasn't fooling the world I was just fooling myself.

Keeping up the appearance of being "just fine" became very tiring. Changes had to be made. I had to make changes in myself. So, my journey began. I started reading books, doing the exercises in the books that I thought would help me and started working with some people. I was seeking the "the magic pill," the "quick fix" and quick-and-easy cure but for me it has not gone that way. I had to do "the work." I had to go through the pain. I had to put the time in. It has transformed me to the person I am today. I don't pretend to be "cured" but I do feel better about myself and I find as I help myself I am able to help others. As a Minister it's very gratifying helping others while I'm helping myself as well.

EXERCISE 13: DO YOU THINK YOU ARE THE REAL YOU OR ARE YOU FOOLING YOURSELF? DO YOU THINK YOU ARE FOOLING OTHER PEOPLE AS WELL? WRITES ABOUT YOUR THOUGHTS ABOUT THESE SUBJECTS.

CHAPTER 14

Meet My Longtime Companion - Suicide

I would like you to meet my longtime companion: Suicide. Suicide started traveling with me since my late teens and early twenties and has been with me on and off ever since. Suicide usually makes his/her presence known when I feel hopeless for a long period of time. When things simply are happening for me or breaking my way, or I don't see a positive future for me. That's when Suicide tends to show up in my life. Suicide feels like a negative, depressing, and a very sad presence when it's me and it makes me feel very hopeless.

I am making light of the subject at hand as a coping mechanism because if I dwell on Suicide too much, I go to places in my mind that I should not go. Very bad places that no one should go alone. Places where I get very sad, depressed and experience a sense of hopelessness. So, I decided to make Suicide a companion on my life's journey. <u>Not a friend but a companion</u>. Someone who comes to visit on occasion and who I would like to leave as soon as possible. I have accepted Suicide as a companion not as a solution to my life but as a chronic "dis-ease" of my Mind, Emotions and Spirit that is in remission. Most of the time but ever so often I have a "flare up" that I have to manage, perform self-care, and deal with when it does happen. The good thing, since I have been working on myself, and with the help of others, is when my companion Suicide does visit, Suicide does not stay as long as he/she used to and does not make me as sad, depressed and hopeless as he/she once did. And for that, I am very grateful.

My acceptance of Suicide doesn't mean I like when Suicide visits, it just means I am in a place where I can "manage my suicidal thoughts versus my suicidal thoughts managing me." For that I am very grateful. The work I have done on myself (and continue to do on myself) continues to pay off, my life is better and getting better all the time. There is hope for me. There is a better life ahead of me. I just don't say it, I feel it and I see it.

Though this book is about my life's journey, it can be about your life's journey as well. No matter where you are in your life, no matter what you are going through, have been through, think you're going to go through, there is always hope. There is always God.

God is in the best of circumstances and God is in the worst of circumstances. Having faith in God is one of the most powerful tools of physical, mental, emotional and spiritual well-being in our toolbox. What is Faith? The definition from the Holy Bible about faith: "Now faith is the substance of things hoped for, the evidence of things not seen." Hebrews 11:1. "Faith is the connecting power into the spiritual realm, which links us with God and makes Him become a tangible reality to the sense perceptions of a person". Faith is the basic ingredient to begin a relationship with God.

Wherever you are in your healing journey, add God to it if you haven't already done so. It doesn't matter if you never believed in God. Or that God has let you down. Just ask God anyway. Start now with Prayer. You don't need any special tools, devices, or locations. Doesn't have to be fancy or poetic or dramatic. Just talk to God like you would be talking to a good friend a very good friend. Start now and if you never prayed let's do it together:

"Dear God, I am in a very bad place in my life because of (fill in the blanks) _____, _____, and _____. Please help me quickly and show me the way to living a better life. I'm looking forward to You helping me in the way that you know is best for me. Thank You God. Amen." This is just a short and simple prayer to God. So, there are no more reasons or excuses that one does not know how to pray to God. Furthermore, there are hundreds if not thousands of free prayers to God and all types of circumstances on the Internet. I have included some prayers in the back of this book for your use and reflection.

EXERCISE 14: HAVE YOU EVER HAD SUICIDAL THOUGHTS? IF SO, WRITE ABOUT THEM IN DETAIL.

PART III

RECOVERY AND REBUILDING

CHAPTER 15

Adulthood

As I mentioned in a previous chapter and worth repeating, television personality, author and now network executive Oprah Winfrey said something on her talk show about 20 years ago or so that has stuck with me until this day. Whether she was quoting someone else I cannot recall at this time. I really did not understand the meaning of what she said at the time but as I have gotten older it has proven itself to be extremely true and I understand the meaning loud and clear now. Oprah said, "Your feelings will wait." How true that phrase has become for me! In order to emotionally survive (and not commit suicide), I buried in my subconscious mind all the pain, anger and sorrow of my childhood and formative years. I did what I had to do to "emotionally survive" in my life. Grew up emotionally faster than I should have, emotionally skipped past my childhood, tolerated, excused and accepted my parents' behavior and did what I had to do my entire life. Worked hard, paid my bills, and was responsible for all the going on in my life and took care of my parents (losing everything in the process) until their respective deaths.

Sure enough as soon as my life started quieting and settling down, my repressed feelings came up and are still coming up, getting in the way of me experiencing my best life. I have been doing the work and continue to do the work to clear all the pain, anger and sorrow in my life but it has taken time and continues to take time. I ask the people I work with "how long is it going to take until this is over?" And I have learned that there is no real answer. The true answer is as it was: it will take what it takes. And that just stinks! Everyone is different. Everyone heals differently. Everyone processes things at a different rate. Everyone has different pain.

I have seen major improvements in my life, my happiness and hope for a bright future have dramatically improved but I'm not there yet. I hope things improve faster than they have been as I get a bit squirrely (mentally stressed) emotionally at times (read Koo-Koo, Crazy, Mashugana, Pick a Word it will fit 😊) but I know intellectually and in my heart that things are working out for me according to God's plan. That too is something I must have faith in, that all is happening in my life for a reason and a purpose that will be revealed to me at the proper time. These words are easy to say and hard to live.

EXERCISE 15: **ANY ISSUES IN YOUR CHILDHOOD AND/OR ADULTHOOD THAT YOU FEEL ARE NOT RESOLVED IN YOUR LIFE? IF SO, WRITE ABOUT THEM IN DETAIL.**

CHAPTER 16

I'm Not Damaged or Broken

For the longest time in my life (and occasionally now) I felt that I was damaged or broken inside, emotionally, in my heart and in my head. Yes, I have been hurt by those I loved; I bear those emotional scars as I have learned to forgive (a long-term process for me) those who have hurt me. While I may forgiven those who have hurt me I don't forget what they did to me and what I allowed to be done to me. I don't forget, especially as those memories warn me that if someone comes into my life and they behave in that same or similar manner, I will not give them a chance to hurt me in that way or any other way for that matter. I don't like to think of myself as paranoid just "more cautious" than I once was when people come into my life and start showing hurtful behaviors towards me. I get rid of them much sooner than later. I take responsibility for the people that come into my life. People are either "assets or liabilities" in my life. I decided to keep the assets and get rid of the liabilities as quickly as possible.

As for feeling broken or damaged, through the work I have done on myself (many of the exercises in this book, working with others, etc.) I am "repairing" the "brokenness" and "damage" feeling I have about myself. It's not a quick fix. As usual, it's taking longer than I think it should. And I should be feeling much better than I am, etc, etc. etc... Truth be told, I am doing better than I once was. I am feeling better than I once was as well. I do think about suicide much less than I used to. Yes, I am feeling good, but I know I still can feel a lot better. That's why I continue to work on myself. I hope that by continuing to work on myself I can help others by example. It's easy to "talk the talk" but "walking the walk" is a different matter. There are no shortcuts, I have to put in the work myself, into myself, if I want to stay well and continue my progress on myself. I'm worth it and you are too.

EXERCISE 16: **DO YOU FEEL "DAMAGED" OR "BROKEN"? IF SO, WRITE ABOUT IT IN DETAIL.**

CHAPTER 17

Breaking the Chains of Pain

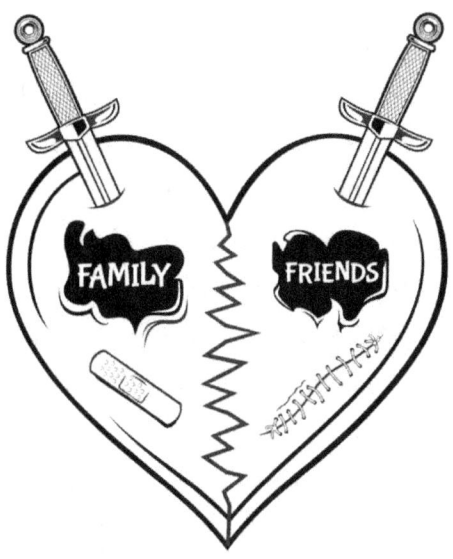

The above image is what my emotional heart looks like to me—full of pain, anger and sorrow. Betrayal from my family (immediate and extended) and close friends. Emotional cuts, wounds, and lies that broke my heart. The scars are all there. They are not visible to the "naked eye" but can be seen and felt by the "emotional heart." While you won't see it on any death certificate that someone "died from a broken heart," people do indeed die from broken hearts and/or at a minimum get sick emotionally or otherwise. I find my "emotional sickness" is also rooted with the abuse I was exposed to as a child in how my parents fought viciously in front of me and the lack of love and nurturing I received in my life, especially in my younger years. I have had to grow up being in "emotional survival" mode mentality to survive or I would have killed myself to escape the emotional pain that I was being subjected to by my parents and the isolation that I was living in. I felt that I was an "emotional prisoner" being restrained with "Chains of Pain."

I had to break the "Chains of Pain" in my family. What are my "Chains of Pain"? Simply put the "Chains of Pain" are family-negative patterns causing emotional pain within the current family unit and future family units and chances are from past family units as well. For me personally, I suspect there was much emotional pain, problems, and issues with both of my parents in their lives and possibly their own parents (my grandparents) which may have extended even further in the ancestral linage. My mother clearly had emotional and other psychological issues. I suspected my father as well but of a different nature. Their emotional issues affected me deeply. Their emotional problems, manifesting as constant fighting which was very traumatic and emotionally damaging for me to have been exposed to as a very young child. While all couples fight sooner or later, there is "fighting" and there is "FIGHTING." The first type of fighting is civilized. Yes, there is some yelling but within a reasonable amount of time things calm down and there is the "making up and apologizing." All is as it was, back to normalcy within the relationship. The second type of "FIGHTING" is very vicious, like wild animals fighting to the death. Like a blood sport. Yelling and screaming that is very cruel, hurtful and painful in nature. Very painful things are said that cannot be unsaid, that cannot be unheard – especially by a young child. These two people, my parents, who were supposed to love and cherish each other, now engaged in what almost appeared to be a fight to the death. How it pains and hurts my heart and soul even to this day, even though they are both dead.

I know that if I would have gotten married at a young age and had children, I too would have repeated the patterns of "Chains of Pain" and would have been abusive to my wife and children. I saw it done in my family growing up, so I would just repeat the negative emotional patterns again and maybe even worse. How? By being emotionally abusive, drinking to excess to deaden the emotional pain, cheating on my wife, or whatever else I could think of to lash out. Furthermore, I did not get married and have children at a young age so as to not expose my precious and beloved family to the "emotional poison and emotional sicknesses" my parents possessed. I was determined to "punish" my parents as they were not to share in the joy of being grandparents or any of my happiness. While it can be argued that in doing so I also punished myself but I will always know in my head, heart and soul that it was the right thing to do as no one, especially loved ones, should be exposed to that type of emotional pain and suffering for any long period of time as I was. I strongly believe it is at the root of all of my emotional pain and suffering in this lifetime. Not coming from a strong, loving and emotionally well-balanced family has been a hindrance to me to this day. Nothing will or has taken the place of the love of a mother and father, which I never had, and never will. Anything that has come close, has only been a faint copy at best. I grieve for the love of my parents that I never had and will never have. This is the hole in my soul that I work on healing.

EXERCISE 17: DO YOU FEEL YOU HAVE AND/OR ARE THERE "CHAINS OF PAIN" IN YOUR FAMILY? IF SO, WRITE ABOUT IT HERE.

CHAPTER 18

Wholeness and "Hole-ness"

For the longest time in my life I did not feel like a "Whole Person," like a fully complete person. At times I still feel that way but understand it is more of a perception issue in my mind than in my reality. I felt more like a "Hole Person," a person with a lot of "holes" in my life. One hole—no brothers and sisters, another hole—no loving family, another hole—no caring extended family, and on and on and on. What I have learned is while these things may be true on the physical plain of existence, in my mind and heart I have grown to have these "holes" filled by various people, events, religious and spiritual practices.

I am not in denial about the reality of my life, but I have changed the perception of things. Dr. Wayne Dyer (Internationally renowned author and speaker in the field of self-development) once said, "Change the way you look at things and the things you look at change." I understand that quote much better now by living it. I am a very independent person by nature. My life and not having certain people in it enables me to live the type of lifestyle I choose. While there are some people missing in my life, other people have filled the "holes" I once thought I had and would hold me back from living a fulfilled life.

I have tried to fill the holes in my life with food, shopping, sex, alcohol and other various distractions only to learn, especially as I have gotten older, that the "holes" in my soul would only be fulfilled only for a short amount of time until the emotional emptiness would come back again. The older I have become, the shorter the time, until it got to the point that within a few minutes from when I filled the holes, the emotional emptiness comes back again.

Deep inside my being I knew that all I had been doing was "treating the symptoms" of my problems (my "holes") and I had to get to the "root cause" if I was going to stop having suicidal thoughts. My self-healing journey began by searching for ways to fill the "holes" in my soul. And when I say, "fill the holes in my soul," I mean heal the holes in my soul. For each hole represents an emotional issue of pain in my life. I started reading all types of books, going to seminars and workshops, and working with spiritual-based counselors and healers. I started to better understand my problems and what I had to do to heal them. It has not been a quick fix, no "magic pill" or potion, just working on myself with various people guiding me along the way. Sometimes I have healed big holes in my soul and sometimes I have healed small holes in my soul. Sometimes the healings have been quickly attained and sometimes it took a while to be healed on a "hole" – with some healings continuing to this day. Sometimes I would feel good after a hole in my soul was healed and sometimes I would feel not so good after a hole was healed. I do know one very important thing for sure that I am not the same person I was when I started my healing journey on healing the holes in my soul, I feel more "whole" (complete) now than I have ever felt before. I still have my bad days but I'm not suicidal when I do have bad days. I'm not quick to go to that dark place in my mind where there is no hope, that place of only darkness where it feels like I am going to end my life. It hasn't been an easy road to healing the holes in my soul but there is much more light in my life than there ever has been in my past. God has provided me with the right people, with the right healings to be done at the right time, and for that I am eternally grateful. God has done all this for me, and God will do it for you as well. Whatever you are going through, whatever you believe is wrong in your life whatever pain and suffering you are experiencing, God will find a way where there appears to be no way. Have faith in God. Get professional help especially if you have addictions and/or other mental/emotional issues. Join 12-step programs, self-help groups and read positive self-help books. Do your best to be strong. Pray, mediate, be of service to others, and good tidings and healings will come your way as well. Whether you are religious or not, believe in God or not, or have just given up on yourself, just say this short simple prayer every morning when you wake up, **"God please help me now. I can't do this alone. I need Your help, Your guidance and Your love. God please show me your love until I can love myself to help heal myself and be hole and complete. Thank you dear God. Amen."** I have said this prayer myself, many times and have been blessed with many healings. I pray the same goodness for you.

EXERCISE 18: **DO YOU FEEL YOU HAVE ANY "HOLES IN YOUR SOUL"? IF SO, WHAT ARE THEY? WRITE ABOUT IT HERE.**

CHAPTER 19

Healing

My healing journey began in my early 20's. In my mind if something is broken it can be fixed. I don't know if that's a guy thing but that's the way my mind works. I knew by then that something wasn't right with me, that something was "broken" (for lack of a better word at the time) and that it had to be "fixed". Again, if it's "broken" it can be "fixed," that's what I thought at the time. I would learn in time that I really was "emotionally wounded" and I needed "healing." Healing is a process that takes time, while fixing, depending on the problem, can be done in a few sessions with the right tools, equipment, parts, etc.

I started with the questions (which I still use today, to a lesser extent) of: Why Me? Why me these emotional wounds? Why me these problems? The answers in time, would come back as: Why NOT you? Why NOT you these emotional wounds? Why NOT you these problems? I would say to myself, "I'm a good person, do good things, help people, etc. Why is this all happening to me?" I really never got an answer to that specific question, but I do suspect, based on my learning about Karma and past lives, that I am working off some bad karma from various past lives in this life. Personally, I need things to make sense in my life. There has to be reason, good or bad, behind everything so it "computes" in my mind. Again, don't know if it's a guy thing but that's the way I'm wired. For example, a jealous wife kills the husband, though a tragic event, I understand why she did it. The situation is resolved in my mind. After years and years (and I mean many years like twenty or so), I started accepting the pain, anger and sorrow (the wounds) of my life and started the letting go process of "Why me?" questions and started concentrating on healing my life.

I really did not know where to turn for help, guidance and healing with this type of situation. Modern medicine, that is, psychiatry didn't seem appropriate as I felt the problem was not with my body or some type of chemical imbalance. I did not understand, know, or whether I could afford the whole concept of "seeing a psychologist." I thought that was only for "rich people with rich people problems." I started with what was available to me at the time. I would get readings at psychic fairs to get an understanding and help of what was going inside me and how I could get help and/or help myself. Keep in mind there was no Internet at the time and information was not as readily available as it is now. Anything I learned was from word of mouth (which is sometimes not that reliable) or through books at the library. One very good thing that has come from the Internet is the wealth of knowledge of the various healing modalities to help people with emotional wounds, coupled with people sharing their stories of their own personal healing journeys. Though I received general guidance from the readings, the readers were not experts in the specific areas that they suggested I needed help with – so my healing journey began. With the healing journey also came my new personal mantra, from "I'm broken, and I need to be fixed" to "I'm emotionally wounded, and I need to heal." What also came out a few times in the readings with various readers is that I am a healer myself. As the saying goes, "physician heal thyself," so I started working on myself as well.

I started working with whoever I felt could help me heal. I

participated in all types of healing modalities. Some of which I questioned if they really did do anything to help heal me. It is said, "no healing ever goes to waste," so I tried many types of healing modalities. Emotional wounds are a bit tricky in that only the person who is wounded really knows if they are completely healed, unlike physical wounds where you see the wound has been healed. I came to learn that my emotional wounds have "layers" to them like an onion (hence the phrase "peeling back the onion") and that I had to heal layers of wounds until I finally got to the main cause of my emotional wound. In my case I had to "heal the symptoms so I could get to the cause." My excessive alcohol consumption in my 20's and 30's wasn't the problem, it was a symptom of my pain, anger and sorrow of my emotional wounds and my attempt to deaden my emotional pain. Since I have healed certain things in my life, I can drink in moderation now without it being a problem, I know when to stop and when I have had enough. I don't fool myself that alcohol can be a "slippery slope" to triggering certain emotions to come up, so I'm very mindful about my consumption. Furthermore, as I have gotten older drinking alcohol doesn't have the "zing" it once had in my life. I can take it or leave and there are weeks I do not consume alcohol or miss not doing so.

As for the healing modalities I have experienced many in my life. Having been told that I am a healer myself, that was even more of an impetus to experience the various type of healing modalities and healers that went along with them.

Just to mention a few here I have worked with: Spiritual Healers, Chiropractors (certain type of Chiropractic adjustments are said to help release trapped emotions in the body), Deep Tissue Massage

Therapist (again to help release emotions trapped in the body), Craniosacral Therapy (again to help release emotions), Reiki Masters, Shamans, and many more. My personal requirement to work with a type of healing and healing practitioner was: 1. My research on that type of healing, 2. What is being told to me and the sincerity of the practitioner wanting to help me, and 3. Is this something that I feel will help me on my healing journey? I must admit that having been told that I was a healer myself I wanted to experience as many reasonable, safe and practical healing modalities that I could and that hopefully will help me and add tools to my "healing tool kit" though a particular healing modality may not work for me, it may help someone else's healing journey.

One of the main healing modalities that helped me was "Soul Retrieval." In her book, <u>Soul Retrieval: Mending the Fragmented Self</u> by Sandra Ingerman, she states that, *"The basic premise is whenever we experience trauma, a part of our vital essence separates from us in order to survive the experience by escaping the full impact of the pain."* For me the process has taken many years and still is not complete, but I can state without any hesitation that I am a noticeably different, stronger and more complete person than I was before the start of my healing journey. Parts of my "soul" were indeed gone from me and were "retrieved" to help me become whole once again. I continue to "retrieve" my "soul fragments" through various healings that I receive and that I continue to become more of a "whole" person once again.

I believe we are born "whole and complete" when we come into this plane of existence and that over time various factors in our upbringing and our lives have an impact on who we become and create the holes in our souls. Examples of these factors include: our birth family, the local environment and all its aspects (physical, mental, emotional, spiritual), our extended families, ancestors and even past lives. We can and may start getting "holes in our souls" intentionally and/or unintentionally, the "holes" may or may not have been inflicted upon us. We may have holes in our souls from past lives that need to be resolved/healed in this life. The parent that abuses their children **because that's the way they were raised**; the alcoholic that drinks to excess **because everyone in his family and friends drinks that much as well**; the boyfriend that verbally abuses and bullies his girlfriend that leads to her drug abuse **because that's how we do things in my culture**. The abuse can take so many different forms: physically, mentally, emotionally and even spiritually. Scars in all their forms are a painful reminder of the pain that was inflicted on an individual at one time or another in their lives. Having sat and experienced many individuals' personal experiences in "the rooms" in 12 step work there are no shortages of personal pain and suffering. It is not difficult to understand why some people turn to alcohol (or drugs) to sooth the pain of the scars they carry. The "holes" in their souls created by their painful experiences usually at the hands of another. We try to fill the "holes in our souls" with alcohol, drugs or whatever only to find out it's a short-term solution and the pain comes back again only to hurt again. I know I have been there myself. All the alcohol in the world could not fill the "holes" in my soul to make me feel "whole" again. I tried even more healings, some healing and healing modalities effects lasted longer than others and that gave me reason to carry on. It gave me hope that I can get better, feel better and be happy regardless of what I have been through in my life. **Sometimes**

hope was the only thing I could hold on to. Sometimes hope was my one and only friend. I have seen, experienced and felt the "darkness" and know what complete despair looks like and it was hope that got me through and into the "light." **Never give up there is always hope.** There is always God. God will make a way where this is no way. God made a way for me. God will make a way for you.

Another healing modality that I experienced and enjoy doing to this day is Shamanism. Shamans (they are both men and women) are extraordinary healers as well as being extraordinary people. Shamanic practitioners work with spiritual beings in other realities to heal people by restoring their spiritual power. Shamans can call on spirits to help restore portions of the soul. A Shaman can also be an aid in physical healing and work, at times, with western medicine practitioners. It is a very healing experience to work with the 4 elements (earth, air, fire and water) as the 4 elements are a part of us. Working the Gaia (Mother Earth), spending time in nature, with the trees, animals, birds, crystals, etc. all have their healing knowledge to share with us if we are willing to learn. When I start to "live in my head a bit too much" I go to nature and become grounded once again. It doesn't matter what type of nature you like: a park, a stream, the mountains, the waters all have grounding properties...it's all good, it all heals.

I continue to work with healers in experiencing different healing modalities. As well as continuing to work with healing all aspects of my being: the physical, the mental, the emotional and the spiritual.

The Physical – I am working on healing my eating habits as I am overweight. The Mental – I am working on eliminating my negative self-talk and other "stinkin' thinkin'". Emotionally – I am working on loving myself in a healthy ego-balanced manner and being of service to other more. Spiritually – I am working on my relationship with God. Though I am a Minister I still occasionally get mad (two-fisted mad) at God and need to make amends and renew my relationship with God.

As I get older I am starting to get a better understanding of the various forms of "Hygiene" required to lead a good life. Hygiene is defined conditions or practices conducive to maintaining health and preventing disease. The forms of hygiene I mean for human beings are in the areas of Physical, Mental, Emotional and Spiritual hygiene. Physical Hygiene is straight forward and that is to bath on a regular basis, consuming healthy foods and liquids, taking care of the body without ingesting too many unnecessary poisons. Mentally – The mind works like a computer, as the saying goes "garbage in – garbage out." So, Mental Hygiene consists of consuming positive, uplifting and hope-filled things like good books, good music, good TV/movies/videos, good conversations. Emotional Hygiene consists of being of service to others, being of service to yourself, as well as by being a good person and taking care of yourself. Spiritual Hygiene consists of having a relationship with something greater than yourself like God, the various Prophets and Saints as well as various spiritual practices like prayer, meditation, and yoga for example.

For me my healing journey continues and I'm finding out that it's more of a journey than a destination. Maybe "the journey" is "the destination." I never really understood what that meant until now. I guess I will continue to heal until the end of my life. That's a very interesting concept, that I will keep on pondering on my healing journey. I'm getting better and feeling better all the time so something good must be happening. I like to think so... ☺.

EXERCISE 19: **DO YOU THINK YOU HAVE AREAS IN YOUR LIFE (PHYSICALLY, MENTALLY, EMOTIONALLY, SPIRITUALLY) THAT NEED TO BE HEALED? IF SO, WRITE ABOUT THEM.**

CHAPTER 20

Forgiveness

What is Forgiveness? It is defined as the action or process of forgiving or being forgiven. For me this has been and continues to be a very important part of my healing – forgiving those that have hurt me, especially my parents. For me it has and continues to be a process. I continue to pull back the layers of pain, anger and sorrow and keep on forgiving, keep on healing. Though I will forgive others for what they have done to me, intentionally or unintentionally, I do not forget. As the saying goes: "Fool me once shame on YOU. Fool me twice shame on ME!" Though I am a Minister and do my best to "talk the talk and walk the walk" of being a Minister, one thing I AM NOT, that is, anyone's doormat to be treated anyway they choose. Whatever it is; my personality, my astrological sign (Leo), my ethnic culture (Italian), life in my family (emotional survival of the fittest), my past lives (as a Warrior) or whatever, one thing that I am extremely clear on is those days are over in my life. I have toughened up emotionally and though still nice, friendly and sociable to all people I do not tolerate people's nonsense, drama or bullshit any longer. I have come to the conclusion, in my life that people who are in and come into my life are either "ASSETS" or "LIABILITIES." By asset I mean add value to my life and not in a financial manner but emotionally. People that are supportive, that are there for me when the going gets tough and can be counted on when you need someone. If I deem a person an asset I will do as much for them as they do for me, to add value in their lives as well. Conversely, if I deem a person a "liability," a user, a hurter of people, a taker more than a giver, an "energy vampire" (sucking the energy out of you with their constant problems and neediness and not giving in return when they can) – THEY'RE OUT! Services no longer required, PINK SLIP time and get out and far away from me as you can. As quickly as you can.

Now for the reality of forgiving as a part of my healing, I continue to deal with this to this day. I have had to forgive people in my life in order to move on to bigger and better things. Not forgiving people, especially my parents, was holding me back, stopping good things from coming into my life. I started noticing the more I forgave them, the more good things started coming my way. I want to be clear, it's not like I read a book, took a seminar, attended a workshop and magically I forgave, and people were forgiven. It has been a process, and a process takes time. While I have forgiven and healed the "big boulders" of pain, anger and sorrow from my parents in my life I am still dealing with the fall out and the minor stuff throughout the healing. I have been fortunate in that I have been guided by God's hand, and my searching, to the right people to work with in my forgiveness and healing journey (as will you once you make the decision to start healing yourself) to release the emotional pain that has held me back from moving forward. The emotional pain had to be released as it was only "growing like a cancer," getting worse as evident by my suicidal thoughts. As I did the work on myself, the forgiveness and healing on myself, the suicidal thoughts subsided as well. The work on myself, the people who helped me, the prayers, the meditations, the helping others, the taking care of myself (physically, mentally, emotionally and spiritually) all were contributors to my mental health and well-being and my attitude toward myself and me not taking my life. I'm not saying it's easy but there is a light at the end of the tunnel. I have had to put the time into my healing and forgiveness of others so I can move forward in my life and I'm worth it...and you are too.

Previously in this book I mentioned an exercise to write a letter (as many times as you need to) to the people you need to forgive in your life and burn it once written, to release them and *you* from the painful attachment you have with them. This is just one of the exercises to help you on your healing journey. If it resonates with you do it, if it does not resonate with you don't do it. Find exercises and practitioners that will help you forgive the people who have done you wrong in your life. The tools are available. It can be done. You can do it. You will move on with your life. You will find happiness. You will find your true self once again. I know that God wants that for you and I strongly believe you want that for yourself and those people around you. Suggested resources will be posted in the back of the book as well.

EXERCISE 20: ARE THERE ANY PERSON(S) YOU NEED TO FORGIVE? DO YOU NEED TO FORGIVE YOURSELF FOR ANYTHING? IF SO, WRITE ABOUT IT IN YOUR NOTE BOOK.

CHAPTER 21

All You Need is Love

As the song goes All You Need is Love (The Beatles)! Love always has been, continues to be, and always will be the answer to so many of life's problems. I also believe that the lack of love always has been, is currently, and always will be the reasons why so many people have issues in their lives. I'm no different. The lack of love in my life has made me who I am today. Yet I continue to marvel as to where I get my ability and strength to have love for others. I do not understand why inside of myself I have the ability to love others, yet I do not have the same love for myself. There was one time I did not like myself and even hated myself. My thinking was that I must be a bad person for all that has happened and continues to happen to me, and that I'm being punished by God and if God hates me it's perfectly acceptable for me to hate myself. Since God hates me and I hate myself it's okay for me to hurt myself in various different ways, drinking and other things that I'm not too proud of in my life. I have come a long way from that thinking. Though I don't hate myself any longer and I'm slowly starting to like myself I still have remnants of that type of thinking in my mind. Loving myself is a bit of a stretch for me right now but I am slowly getting there through proper self-care and nurturing. As the saying goes, "I must teach the things that I must learn myself."

As for loving one's self what I mean here is a healthy love of self and not a narcissistic (vain, self-absorbed, egotistic) type of love. How can you have love for others if you do not have a healthy love for yourself? If one has love for oneself then why would someone want to commit suicide? Is it that lack of a healthy self-love that drives one to suicide? God loves us so much that we have been given the gift of "free will," but this **does not** mean that we can use this free will to take our own lives. Although having experienced the lack of love in my life and now come to empathize with those in the same situation, this is neither a reason or an excuse to end one's life. If a person does not have love in their lives, neither from family, friends or of oneself, does their lives have no meaning? The short answer is no, of course not and their lives still have meaning. The long answer is discussed in the following chapters.

EXERCISE 21: DO YOU HAVE A HEALTHY LOVE OF YOURSELF? WHY OR WHY NOT? DO YOU LOVE OTHERS? WHY OR WHY NOT? WRITE OUT YOUR THOUGHTS ABOUT THESE SUBJECTS.

CHAPTER 22

The Animal Kingdom

God in God's infinite wisdom, besides creating humankind, has created the animal kingdom. Besides being a source of physical nutrition for human beings, they are also a source of emotional and spiritual support to us all. In the previous chapter I discussed the concept of love and sometime not having love in our lives for various reasons. God has created animals, specifically domesticated pets, that love humans unconditionally. I like to think that is God is manifesting in physical form to show us love. I am always amazed that you can take the most unlovable person and put them with a loving pet and this "Scrooge-like" person becomes a big "mush-ball" of an individual in no time at all. The ability of pets to bring out the best in humans is a just a wonderous thing.

Why am I bringing up animals while discussing the pain of lack of self-love? The animal kingdom, in all its forms, from the mighty lion who's the king of the jungle to the tabby cat that's in the local animal pound are our "helpers" in this life. They are here to help all of us on our spiritual journeys. From helping us to find the love we have for ourselves and others ("emotional helpers and healers") to being sacred messengers ("spiritual helpers") from the spirit world to help us on our spiritual paths. If you're having difficultly finding love within yourself, go spend some time at the local animal shelter and watch "the magic" happen all by itself.

As for me and animals, though I have never owed a pet myself I have found much comfort in being with other people's pets, going to and supporting pet shelters and the spiritual healing with various "spirit animals" (in certain spiritual traditions or cultures, "spirit animal" refers to a spirit which helps, guide, or protects a person on a journey and whose characteristics that person shares or embodies). The spirit animals give me a sense of peace and serenity in my life that I did not know existed. The animals that I have experienced in my spiritual journey have been: the White Lion, the Bear and the Horse. Each spirit animal has unique qualities that enhance my own abilities. The animals, in all their forms, are yet another way that I feel I am connected to the whole and that I am not apart from the whole, but I am indeed connected to the whole and in being so feel a stronger connection to God. In the next section I will share how we can further connect to God.

EXERCISE 22: **DO YOU OWN A PET OR ANIMALS? IF NOT, SPEND SOME TIME A LOCAL ANIMAL SHELTER OR ANIMAL SANCTUARY. WRITE ABOUT YOUR EXPERIENCES AND HOW THE ANIMALS MAKE/MADE YOU FEEL.**

CHAPTER 23

Mother Nature

There is a saying that goes: "If you want to speak to God then **Pray** and if you want to hear God then **Meditate**." Though I have been blessed to feel God's love, I, like the rest of humankind, have never seen God. However, when I am in nature I can sense God's presence in the trees, the streams, and all of nature's majesty. Everything in nature makes sense. Everything in nature has a purpose. Everything in nature has a reason for being, as do we all – a reason for being here, a reason for being.

Any time things stop making sense in my life I go into nature for a few hours. It does not have to be a big deal. Anywhere I am, there is usually a park, beach, lake, stream, or whatever and I just sit and "unplug my brain" and listen. In no time at all, after I have neutralized all the static noise in my head, I can hear the birds singing, and if I'm near a pod, the fish "glub glubbing" and squirrel or chipmunk running in the leaves.

Why is nature so important to our wellbeing? It is another way to "disconnect" our minds for a short while from the fast pace manner in which modern-day life has swept us all. By connecting to nature and we can put all things and our lives into proper perspective. It is another manner to connect to the whole… another way to connect to God. There is such wonder and amazement in nature. We are all connected in nature. There is such wonder and amazement in all of us. We are all connected to each other. We are all connected to God. If God is love and we are all connected to God, then we should all have love for ourselves. And if we hurt inside, then God must hurt inside as well, but God has the answer for that hurt we have inside by healing us with God's love. I have felt the pain inside my heart and soul, and I have felt God's healing love. You can too.

EXERCISE 23: **GO SPEND TIME IN NATURE. START BY TURNING EVERYTHING ELECTRONIC OFF FOR 5 MINUTES, THEN 10 MINUTES AND SO ON. WRITE ABOUT YOUR EXPERIENCES.**

CHAPTER 24

Gratitude

Gratitude has become more important to me as I have gotten older. I had and still have much to be grateful for, but I did not realize that at earlier ages in my life. When I think about all that I am grateful for, there is neither the time or the space to be depressed, sad and worst of all have suicidal thoughts. Though I have not yet lived the life I desired, I have noticed there are those who have things a lot worse than I do. Though (luckily) there is not a "misery index" in life I have learned, and thus I continue to learn about gratitude and how really good my life is.

What am I grateful for? From the basic things in life that so many people do not have. The most important thing of all that I am extremely grateful for is good health. Though my health is not perfect (as I needed to lose weight), for the most part my health is good. I have experienced the type of sickness and pain that one would rather die than go through. I have been fortunate the sicknesses in my life have resolved themselves in relatively short order. I have been with people that have poor health and it's a nightmare that does not end. Waking up in the morning in pain, the whole day in pain and then going to sleep in pain and that's if they can sleep. Many times, the pain even invades the person's sleep. I have been there myself as I had a bout of **sciatica** several years ago that left me waking like a hunchback and racked with so much pain that I could not sleep at night until the pain resolved itself.

What am I grateful for? I am grateful that all my senses work. That I can see, hear, taste, touch, and smell. I notice that there are many people who do not have all their senses or they are losing their senses for whatever reason. What a burden it must be to have lost some of your main senses? I observe the loss of senses in others and it gives me pause in my own life. What would my life be like if I was missing some of my senses?

What am I grateful for? I'm grateful that my mind still works and that I'm able to think clearly. I am grateful that I am able to write and help others through my writing. I am grateful that the negative thoughts I once had rarely come back and when they do come back they rarely last long. I am grateful that my mind is a positive tool and not my enemy any longer.

I am grateful for the people in my life, even those that have hurt me in the past. Obviously I am more grateful for the good people in my life as they give me strength to deal with the adversity in my life and to keep moving on. I must acknowledge those people that have hurt me, as they gave me the impetus (motivation, momentum, push) to help pick myself up, heal, and move on with my life.

I never really valued gratitude before as much as I appreciate things now. Having learned to be grateful for good health especially when I am sick. I have learned to appreciate time especially now that I have recently turned 60 and how quickly time goes by. Turn around once I'm 20, turn around twice I'm 40, and now turn around three times I'm 60. Be grateful for the things you do have and work on the things you want to change.

Why am I talking to you about gratitude? Take personal inventory of your own life. And yes things may not be that way you want them but start with the good things in your life and then start working on the things you want to change. Ask for help from others and remember always to ask for help from God. God is always ready to help. God is always listening. God is always loving you.

EXERCISE 24: **WHAT ARE YOU GRATEFUL FOR IN YOUR LIFE? WRITE YOUR THOUGHTS ABOUT GRATITUDE. WRITE AND WRITE SOME MORE. DO THIS EXERCISE SEVERAL TIMES UNTIL YOU FEEL GRATITUDE IN YOUR LIFE.**

CHAPTER 25

The Spirituality of Suicide - The Spiritual Law of Karma and Other Realities of Life Before Life

As an Inter-Faith (All-Faiths Minister), a man of God, I feel it's my responsibility to discuss the subject matter in this chapter as I would be failing humankind not to mention the spiritual ramifications of suicide (the taking of one's own life). This is knowledge I have acquired over the years (studying various religious beliefs, reading sacred texts, and speaking to people of various religions and spiritual backgrounds), that is available to everyone, as this same message has appeared over and over again to me that it cannot be discounted as mere superstition, religious fanaticism, or myth. The message is that we **ARE NOT TO COMMIT SUICIDE** as there are consequences to the individual soul if he or she does take their life. The person that commits suicide will come back (reincarnate) and there is no guarantee when coming back that their life circumstances will be the same. Meaning that when a soul does come back, they may end up in even worse circumstances than they had before committing suicide. We all come here to learn certain soul lessons until we reach the point in our evolutions where the soul has no need to come back any longer.

There are certain spiritual principles that apply to all of us human beings regardless if an individual accepts them or not, as there are certain physical principles that apply to us all as well. In this chapter I will be discussing the concept of the "Soul Contract," the "Law of Karma," and the Universal Spiritual laws.

What is the Soul Contract? Soul contract(s) are agreements we make with other souls before we are born. The souls we have contracts with will be those souls that bring deep changes into our lives through a unique connection (e.g. Father, Mother, Siblings, Husband/Wife, Boyfriend/Girlfriend, Friends, etc.). These contracts are made with a special purpose, and that is to teach us important lessons we've chosen to learn before reincarnation. So, if a person commits suicide and the soul contract is not complete, the soul must come back until there is completion of said contract. Furthermore, it affects the other souls that you had a contract agreement with. For example, if you had soul contracts with your father and mother to teach you certain soul lessons and you commit suicide, the lessons both you and your parents were supposed to teach each other do not happen and you will have to reincarnate again until the soul lessons are learned. While on the physical plane you would be emotionally hurting and devasting your parents, as well as other family members and friends as well.

There is a certain "spiritual responsibility" we all have to God, the Universe and family members regarding our lives. And while no one has died and come back from being dead (to the best of my knowledge) said these concepts and words, it has been an eternal concept that "what we reap we shall sow" also known as the "Law of Cause and Effect" also known as "The Spiritual Law of Karma." "Karma" is a Sanskrit (an ancient language which used to be spoken in India and is now used only in religious writings and ceremonies) word that roughly translates to "action." It is a core concept in some Eastern religions. "Karma" is defined by the Merriam-Webster dictionary as "The force generated by a person's actions held in Hinduism and Buddhism to perpetuate transmigration and in its ethical consequences to determine the nature of the person's next existence". Furthermore, Wikipedia goes on to say, "It also refers to the spiritual principle of "cause and effect" where intent and actions of an individual (cause) influence the future of that individual (effect). Good intent and good deeds contribute to good karma and happier rebirths, while bad intent and bad deeds contribute to bad karma and bad rebirths."

Sometimes Karma happens quickly, and sometime Karma takes longer to manifest. We have all witnessed an event where someone was wronged and within minutes the person responsible for that wrong behavior is wronged themselves. One example seen often is while driving. A driver cuts someone off on a highway only to be cut off themselves a few moments later – instant Karma! The person that steals from others only to have things stolen from them. The list is endless.

In the next section is a discussion on the Spiritual Law of Karma and all the 12 Spiritual Laws associated with it. Some people might think and/or believe, that while they are neither religious or spiritual that the Spiritual Law of Karma does not really exist, does not pertain to them, or is just a bunch of new age, spiritual "mumbo-jumbo" and they are not concerned about it and they can do want they want without any repercussions, consequences and the like. What if those same people are wrong? What if the Law of Karma really does exist? Then what?

What exactly is the Spiritual Law of Karma and the 12 Spiritual Laws that go with it? As previously defined, Karma is basically the "Law of Cause and Effect" and the corresponding components (or laws) that go with it. Let's have a closer examination of Karma and all that's associated with it. Below is a clear and concise discussion on the Law of Karma and the spiritual laws associated with it:

THE 12 LAWS OF KARMA BY [1]

The 12 Laws of Karma:

1. The Great Law -

Sometimes also called "the Law of Cause and Effect." The Great Law basically says in order to get the things we want, we must also impress those things. The message here is like that of the Law of Attraction. In other words, whatever you give out is also what you will receive, whether it is positive or negative.

2. The Law of Creation

According to the Karmic Law of Creation, we need to be active participants in our lives if we want to get what we desire. We cannot simply wait for things to happen to us.

3. The Law of Humility

Out of the 12 laws of Karma, Buddhism can be seen as often emphasizing the importance of the Law of Humility. What you need to remember about this Karmic rule is that you need to accept the true reality of something before you'll ever be able to change it.

4. The Law of Growth

The message here is that you need to expect a change of yourself before you expect it of the world around you. You only have control over yourself. You use this control that shapes how the universe responds to you.

5. The Law of Responsibility

Karma is often thought of in terms of The Law of Responsibility. It's helpful to remember that you are the source of what happens throughout your journey. What is happening around you is a mirror image of what is happening within you; that is the sense in which you are responsible for all of your life experiences, whether pleasant or unpleasant.

6. The Law of Connection

This law emphasizes the interconnected nature of the past, present, and future, and reminds us that our control over the present and future can help us to obliterate the bad energy of the past (whether it is from our current life or a previous life).

7. The Law of Focus

You will do better in life if you can follow a single train of thought to the exclusion of others. Our minds are not equipped to follow multiple trains of thought with equal competency.

8. The Law of Giving and Hospitality

This law teaches that if you believe a certain thing, then you will naturally be called upon at some stage to demonstrate your commitment to that truth. The focus here is on the link between belief and practice.

9. The Law of Here and Now

In Buddhism, Karma is connected to ideas about accepting the truth of your reality. Equally, Buddhists typically links Karma to the theme of truly living in the present moment. If you cling too hard to past feelings, experiences, and beliefs, you will always have one foot in the past.

10. The Law of Change

This is about connecting with the message that the universe gives us what we need. You will find that history continually repeats itself until you demonstrate that you've learned what you need to in order to create a different future.

11. The Law of Patience and Reward

This law claims that all of your greatest successes require consistent hard work. This means that you need to be patient, regardless of your goals in life.

12. The Law of Significance and Inspiration

This is a good law to reflect on when you need a motivational boost or start to feel like you don't matter. This particular aspect of Karma stresses that every contribution you make will influence the *whole*, however small or great that contribution may be. Whenever you make creative and loving contributions to the world around you, your act inspires similarly positive behavior from others and attracts more positivity back into your life.

What are the Spiritual Consequences of Suicide?

With all that has been discussed in this chapter, what are the Spiritual Consequences of Suicide? We all have been given the gift of "Free Will" that means we have the ability to take our own life if we choose, **HOWEVER** we must be aware of the consequences and the responsibility we have to ourselves, our families, friends and to God and to every single person whose life we would have touched in a significant way if we make that irreversible choice. What if YOU, and only YOU, is the person that is to help a child become the next doctor to cure cancer? How? Maybe that child was supposed to be born through YOU. Maybe that child is in a family that was cold, insensitive and uncaring and YOU are the extended family member, friend, neighbor, etc. that was always there for this child to give encouragement, guidance, and love. And because this child did not get these things from YOU, the child did not become a doctor, did not cure cancer and even more people suffered and died all because YOU killed yourself. Yes, the possibilities are endless. Stick around. YOU don't kill yourself. YOU get help. YOU have options. YOU have hope. There are many, many options to get help. YOU can and will make a positive difference in other people's lives. As YOU have been helped, YOU will help others. YOU can always ask God for help. God is ALWAYS LISTENING. God will find a way for YOU where there appears to be no way. Trust God. God believes in YOU and YOU need to believe in yourself!

What if this is all nonsense? And what if it is NOT nonsense and this is ALL REAL? Then what???

As for me, as I previously mentioned, by studying the various religions, having read many books, gone to lectures, watched videos, etc. on the subject of Karma and having been told by ascended beings directly (through channeled readings) and indirectly (through their writings), I now know the consequences if I should commit suicide. They all have told me in no uncertain terms that if I should kill myself that I will be coming back to this planet to complete my soul's journey and contracts and when I do come back there is no guarantee that my life's circumstances will be as good as they currently are now and I could end up in worse circumstances, much worse, filled with even more emotional pain and suffering than I have now! Being the annoying "know it all" that I sometimes can be, I said back to them, what if I come back and I end up in better circumstances than I am now and they all said to me the same thing: "You won't. It most likely will be even worse." Normally I would just shrug it off, but I asked the same question to other ascended beings over the past 30 years and they all said the same thing. I personally, can have or make no excuses should I commit suicide and when I am met on the other side by whoever meets me, GOD, Jesus, etc. There can never be "I was never told or warned about the consequences of my actions" for me. I will have no excuses. So, for me these words I write are very real, not just drama or fantasy. I still am human, have my emotional pains, have my tough days and some days are tougher than others and those thoughts of suicide occasionally come to mind and I too must do the things I tell others to do and I too ask God for help and luckily I too see that God finds a way for me where there appears to be no way.

The following was told to me from an Ascended Master through a spiritual medium: **"There is no escape from our spiritual path. It is better to heal now then suffer more later."** I hold these words very close to my own heart, mind, and spirit. Though sometimes I don't like or want to hear the truth, the wisdom in what was said to me simply cannot be ignored. I pass these words on to all who will hear them and listen to what needs to be done. It was also told to me that: **"No soul is to leave before their time."** We all came down here to do our own respective *"work"*. We all have a very unique purpose on this planet and that purpose is to be fulfilled before we leave. All of us came here to do something important with our lives, make a difference, and make the world a better place. **Important** in this case does not have to mean curing cancer but if that is your purpose that's not a bad thing either. **Important** means making a positive difference in other peoples' lives. The person that runs a small-town diner may not be curing cancer, but that person does provide a place where people gather for some home-cooked food, fellowship and the excess food that's not sold is donated to the local soup kitchen. Is that person going to change the way the Earth revolves the Sun? No, however what that person is doing is feeding people, helping people, and giving people a hand up while other people that are receiving his food at the local food pantry are going through difficult times. We all are here to make a positive difference in the world, it doesn't always have to be a big production, but it has to help others in one way or another.

I'm a big believer in "Rule of 3." When I hear something 3 or more times, from 3 or more different people, at different times and different places, I believe it. Sometimes, as a Minister, as I have previously mentioned, I feel I'm not like "regular people" and God likes me better because I work for God directly, boy am I wrong, so very wrong. Every spiritual/universal law affects me, pertains to me, just as much as it does to every other person in this world. My additional challenge and responsibility as a Minister is I just can't just "talk the talk" I have to "walk the walk." Meaning whatever I tell others to do I must do it and live it myself, so I know it takes effort and it's hard at times and can be <u>very</u> hard at times. There is a saying, "We teach what we must learn ourselves" and I myself am learning; as I am teaching others, I am also healing myself. As it says in that famous commercial, "I'm not just the president of Acme Hair Club, I'm also a client."

<u>EXERCISE 25:</u> ASK GOD FOR HELP IF YOU ARE FEELING SUICIDAL THEN CONTACT YOU'RE YOUR DOCTOR AND/OR MENTAL HEALTH CARE PROFESSIONAL AND/OR CALL THE SUICIDE HOTLINE. IF YOU'RE NOT FEELING SUICIDAL WRITE A LETTER HELPING SOMEONE WHO IS AND MAIL IT TO THE SUICIDE PREVENTION HOT LINE AND ASK THAT IT BE FORWARDED TO SOMEONE THAT NEEDS HELP.

CHAPTER 26

Discovering Our Life's Purpose – The Journey Within

I truly believe that one reason that contributes to why some people may decide to commit suicide is that they have neither found and/or are not living their true life's purpose. As I have mentioned previously, we are all here for a reason and purpose. Though there may be many reasons why we are here and have incarnated on this planet at this place and this time, I believe one main reason is to help others in one form or another. And yes, to work out Karma from past lives as well. For now, let's concentrate on our life's purpose. I believe we all know what we are here to do, I suspect it is hardwired with all of us and that sometimes we may need some help in discovering our life's purpose.

You may be thinking, "What is your life purpose Reverend Rusty?" My life's purpose is that of a Teacher, Healer, and most important of all, being a Minister and helping, guiding and ministering to all people that seek help. I am most content, fulfilled and happy when I am living my life's purpose. I believe that having a life purpose is so important to our overall well being that I have written a book about it titled: *"Discovering Your Life Purpose: The Journey Within - The True Guide to Achieving Unlimited Happiness, Prosperity and Personal Fulfillment"*. I have enclosed the first chapter of the above for your review:

Chapter 1: Introduction

Since the beginning of humankind, after man's search for food, lodging and procreation he/she started wondering – What am I doing here? What is the purpose of my existence? Should I be doing something in particular with my life? These questions and many more has bothered humankind for eons, so why should today, in this time and this place be any different?

Your journey, should you decide to accept it (and I hope that you do ☺), is to find your life purpose. It may be challenging at times, in so many different ways, to discover your life purpose; however, it is in you nonetheless. It is truly a process of discovery. It is a process of discovering your real self, your true self, the self that is you in this time and in this place. The process will challenge you in ways known and unknown to you; but I will guarantee you, once you have found your life's purpose, your life's true mission, you will never be the same again! Your life will be elevated to a whole new level—one of joy, peace and prosperity!

This book will give you all the necessary tools you need to discover and implement your life purpose. Some of the tools may not be new to you, while others will open your perception in a whole new way. Other methods, tools, and techniques will take you places you have never been before. You will be learning new things, relearning not-so-new things and be opening your mind, body and spirit to the most wonderful adventure of your life! The journey to your life's purpose! The journey to discovering why you are really here!

We will be discussing the tangible and intangible aspects of discovering your life's purpose. We will start with the *creative* and end up with the *concrete*. This resource is designed to give you "practical and proven" tools for you to discover, achieve, and live your life's purpose. This book or I should call it a "Lifebook" has tools, methods, and techniques that are used in the "real" world to help you make a living once you have discovered your life's purpose and achieve all the prosperity you need, want and desire.

Your journey will begin with **Chapter 2: Why Are We Here On This Beautiful Planet?** Start your trip with some reflection as to the reason we are here in the first place. In **Chapter 3: Being Human – What Does It Really Mean?** We'll explore briefly the individual components of being human and how they are "interdependent" upon one another. **Chapter 4: Some Exercises to Make Your Creativity Flow!** Here are some practical exercises to help you along your journey to make it as easy and effortlessly as possible. In **Chapter 5: A Little Bit of Spiritual Stuff To Help You On Your Journey.** We are more than just flesh and bones, we will learn ancient tools to help achieve your life's purpose. **Chapter 6: Guidance Finding Your Purpose from Some Universal Sources.** Whether you believe in a Higher Power or not there are others that can help you on your path. **Chapter 7: Prosperity: What Is the True Meaning?** Though we all want money and lots of it, it's only one piece of being truly prosperous. **Chapter 8: What's Your Passion?** What gets your "motor running" and gets you excited just talking about? We'll spend some time to explore that here. **Chapter 9: How Would You Like to Live Your life?** If you had your choice of doing anything you want, what would it be? Let's look into that here. **Chapter 10: Finding Your Path to Where You Want To Go?** It's time to discuss the reality of where you are now, to, getting where you want to be. In some cases, it may not be as hard as you think! **Chapter 11: What Are Your Personal Gifts, Talents, and Attributes?** We all have them.

Let's start writing them down and evaluate how they can help you on your journey. **Chapter 12: Discover Your Education and Skill Sets?** It's time to take an inventory of your education and skills. You may just be surprised. You may know a lot more than you think you do! **Chapter 13: Your True Job – Learn How to Find It!** You will be surprised to find how people actually got their ideal job. Learn some proven and innovative techniques to land your dream job. **Chapter 14: Yes, You Can Have a Job And Do Your Life Purpose!** Sometimes it may not be a job that will fulfill your life's purpose. We'll examine the options here. **Chapter 15: Should I Be an Entrepreneur?** Running your own business may be another option to achieving your life's purpose. It may just be the right thing for you. **Chapter 16: Your Life Purpose Statement – Let the World Know Who You Really Are!** Start telling the world why you are here and what your life purpose is. How exciting a moment this is in your life! **Chapter 17: Your Life Master Plan – Planning Your Work and Working Your Plan.** It's time to get out there and make it happen. Once you have a plan it's just a matter of execution. **Chapter 18: You Are Instilled with the Power To Manifest the Perfect Life Experience.** Learn a tool to help you achieve all you can be. **Chapter 19: Enjoy and Celebrate Your Life Purpose and Celebrate Your Life!** Congratulations!

What's your life's purpose? If you haven't found your life purpose you're missing out on the real you. You're missing out on your true work. People are waiting for you! Find your life's purpose and watch your life never be the same again!

EXERCISE 26: WHAT'S YOUR LIFE'S PURPOSE? IF YOU KNOW THEN WRITE WHAT IT IS AND WHAT YOU ENJOY ABOUT YOUR LIFE'S PURPOSE. IF YOU DON'T KNOW YOUR LIFE PURPOSE YET THEN FIND A BOOK OR TWO ON THE SUBJECT TO HELP YOU FIND YOUR TRUE LIFE PURPOSE.

CHAPTER 27

God Will Help Us

Having been raised Catholic, I always believed that God lived in a building with a Christian cross on top and that God was a man (God the Father). I found it interesting that God had so many houses all over the place. As I got older I still believed in God, but God was something that was "over there" and "in that building" and one went to "go visit God" to speak with God.

Then in my mid-twenties I had, what I can only describe as a "supernatural experience" with what I believed to be God, it was an indescribable encounter, I sensed "a being" and/or energy source that radiated unconditional love towards me. It was such a gentle, kind and perfect love that continues to move me to this day when I think about it. The experience only lasted for what seemed a few moments, but it changed me forever. I hope everyone experiences God's love in their lifetime.

From that time on I knew God is real and that God does not live in a only in certain buildings and that God exists in each and every one of us. Whether I quote the Holy Bible, "I and the Father are One" (John 10:30 (New International Version)) or I believe in the God-Spark (in Gnosticism and other Western mystical traditions. The divine spark is the portion of God that resides within each human being) also known as the Three-Fold Flame, I believe God to be a real entity. I also believe God to be neither male nor female but both. Again, while raised Catholic it was always "God the Father" in the past few years I believe God to be "God the

Father and God the Mother" all one entity, no duality. While some people believe God does not exist I choose to believe that God DOES exist. Many will argue that if there is a God, one Supreme Being, why does God allow all the suffering in the world? It is my opinion that God has given us all the gift of free will and unfortunately many people choose to use this gift of free will to hurt others rather than helping others. Yet other people will say prove to me that God exists, and my answer is prove to me that God DOES NOT exist. There are so many unexplained miracles that are taken for granted daily: the birth of a child, the working of the human body, and countless other events that have no logical explanations. Are they all just coincidences? I believe not. As for me, having experienced God's love firsthand, I believe in a Supreme Being, the Creator of all things, and that in time all will be revealed to us if we choose to ask the questions and listen for the answers.

Being a Minister I believe myself to be one of God's representatives on this Earth and that one of my duties is to help people understand and work with God. God wants to help us but having given us the gift of free will we "must ask for help." It's not hard to ask for help. The best way I found to ask God for help is while *praying*.

What is Prayer? Prayer is said to be an invocation or act that seeks to activate a rapport with an object of worship through deliberate communication. Praying helps center and quit the mind, body and spirit and helps produce prayers that are meaningful and come from the heart. Meditation complements prayer as it is said; "If you want to talk to God you *Pray* and if you want to hear God's answer you *Meditate*." God will always come to our assistance though not necessarily in the manner we may think. There is a story with a moral that goes...there once was a Minister that asked God for help while there was a flood in his town. As the water started to rise in the town, the local fire department sent a truck to save the Minister, but the Minister refused and told the fire department that "God will save me" so they left. The waters continued to rise to the point that the first floor was completely submerged. Next, the local coast guard arrived with a boat to rescue the Minister, but the Minister once again stated "God will save me" and they too left the Minister. The flooding waters were at the roof and the State Troopers were dispatched by helicopter to rescue the Minister and yet again the Minister said, "God will save me" and they too left the Minister. The next day the Minister drowned and was immediately dispatched to Heaven to meet with God. The Minister asked God, "God have I not been a loyal, loving servant and the shepherd of your people all of my days? God said, "Yes you have been my beloved child." Then the Minister asked God, "Then why did you not rescue me from the flood that took my life?" And God replied, "My beloved child, I sent you a truck, a boat, and a helicopter to rescue you..." The moral of the story is when you ask God for help, God will decide the manner in which God will help you. Sometimes the manner in which God will send help will be even better than the manner in which you needed to be helped in the first place. After you ask God through your heartfelt prayers – let go and let God do what God does in God's way. Don't give up. Keep praying, keep asking, and remember to let go and let God.

Below are some simple prayers that were mentioned in this book (as well as a new one that I added) that I have placed them here again to get you started on your prayer life with God. There are plenty more *free prayers* on the Internet and in prayer books of all sorts.

"God please help me now. I can't do this alone. I need Your help, Your guidance and Your love. God please show me your love until I can love myself to help heal myself and be hole and complete. Thank you dear God. Amen."

"Dear God, I am in a very bad place in my life because of (fill in the blanks) _____, _____, and _____. Please help me quickly and show me the way to a better life. I'm looking forward to You helping me in the way that you know is best for me. Thank You God. Amen."

"Beloved God I honor your Holy Name please hear my prayers, requests and supplications to you. Find a way for me where there appears to be no way. Please help me with the following problems and issues in my life: (fill in the blanks) _____, _____, and _____. You know the best way to help me. Please send your help as soon as possible. Thank you dear God. Amen"

Start your prayer life with God daily and watch your life change in a positive manner. In a relatively short time your life will improve.

EXERCISE 27: WRITE YOUR OWN PERSONAL PRAYER TO GOD. WRITE IT DOWN HERE.

CONCLUSION

It's Not the End It's a New Beginning

This book has been a healing journey for me, and I sincerely hope that those who read it may find tools, insight and most of all hope on their own personal healing journey. Many people may not agree, understand, or support what is in this book and the manner in which I have dealt with the trials and tribulations of my life but then again this has been my healing journey and not theirs.

I have had many personal situations in my life that have brought me to this place. In looking back at my life, I suppose if I did not go through the things I did I would not be the person I am today. Though I <u>did not like</u> my parents I learn to <u>have love for both of them</u>, something that I still struggle with to this day. My journey as an only child has been and continues to be very difficult at times with very few really understanding the true impact it has had and continues to have on me. Yet all of my experiences, the good, the bad and the ugly, have in their own made me stronger. Though it is said "what doesn't kill you makes you stronger" it still has been a tough way for me to grow as an individual.

I continue to deal, on occasion, with my own suicidal thoughts, but the good thing is that they rarely come as often as they used to, don't last as long, and I'm not inclined to act on them. I attribute this to my faith in God, and all the work I have done on myself and continue to do on myself and the people I work with. Also, I do want to stick around for the "good stuff" 😊. Knowing what

I know about suicide I don't have any excuses if I do something foolish like taking my own life. I have been told, as I continue to be healed and I have written about it, I "have talked the talk and now I must walk the walk." Now I must live it, be grateful for each day and help others as I have been helped. I find much personal reward in helping others as I am confident that those who read this book will find helpful tools as well. Having always found that when I help others I am also helping myself. When I made the decision to become a Minister I did not hear the voice of God or experience some mystical apparition I just felt that it was the right thing to do for me. Having more questions than my Catholic faith had answers for, that started my spiritual journey in becoming an Inter-Faith (as mentioned previously I prefer the term All-Faiths) Minister. I have experienced and continue to experience so many wonderous things on my spiritual journey that I must stick around and experience more of them, learn and teach others before I transition. This is my purpose. This is my true work. This is who I really am. And when the time comes and I am in the light of who I AM, and I believe I am one with God and God is living through me and I am living through God. For that reason, when I have my bad moments I fight to stay here. It sometimes truly is a fight. So you fight too!

Suicide is always an option in life and I humbly hope that people do not pursue it. Yes, life can be very hard at times, but I suspect if we do not know hardships how can we truly understand and appreciate the goodness of life. I do believe in a universal God, The Creator, that does not give us more than we can handle. I do believe that there is help from God, directly and indirectly, when we are going through difficult times. I do believe that we must ask for help when we need it. Who to ask? Start with God, through prayer and meditation, your doctor and other mental health professionals, as well as the resources in this book. Though it may feel like it at times...we are never alone. We never have been alone. And we will never be alone. God is always with us. God is in us. We just have to ask God to guide us through the turbulent times in our lives.

As a Minister and a fellow human being, I am saddened every time I hear of another suicide. It does not matter who it is, someone I never knew or some that is well known. I wonder what if this person did not commit suicide? What if this person's destiny was to make a positive impact in the world? What if this person was going to be an instrumental person in curing cancer, solving world hunger, or helping with world peace? What if? The world will never know for they are no longer with us in this beautiful world.

As a Minister I think and ponder on things especially when I see people suffering regardless what type of suffering it is: physical, mental, emotional or spiritual. Some *suffering* can be seen, others cannot. I have experienced both, so I understand the pain. Whether the pain is seen or unseen I assure you it hurts, nonetheless. In so many ways, we as humans have come so far, yet people still are living and dying on the streets, are still hungry and are still hurting. People are still suffering. We live in a world of millions (if not billions) of people living together in a small amount of space yet we are probably some of the loneliest people in modern times. While technology is producing many miracles to help humankind, more and more people are living isolated lives. Though you'll never see this on any death certificate, people do die of "broken hearts" of being hurt by loved ones intentionaly or unintentionally. Though I can't take away the pain of the world, I can do my best to help others in pain. I do know that it starts with me keeping "my side of the street clean (working of myself)" and by doing so I can be an example for others. It's not easy at times but it is the right thing to do.

I would like to share a line from a poem that keeps me going through my challenging times. This line especially, from the poem by John Greenleaf Whittier, says, "Rest if you must but don't you quit" (the entire poem is below).

Don't Quit
by
John Greenleaf Whittier

When things go wrong as they sometimes will,

When the road you're trudging seems all up hill,

When the funds are low and the debts are high

And you want to smile, but you have to sigh,

When care is pressing you down a bit,

<u>Rest if you must, but don't you quit</u>.

Life is strange with its twists and turns

As every one of us sometimes learns

And many a failure comes about

When he might have won had he stuck it out;

Don't give up though the pace seems slow—

You may succeed with another blow.

Success is failure turned inside out—

The silver tint of the clouds of doubt,

And you never can tell just how close you are,

It may be near when it seems so far;

So stick to the fight when you're hardest hit—

It's when things seem worst that you must not quit.

THIS POEM IS IN THE PUBLIC DOMAIN.

Until we meet again
God and I send you love...

RESOURCES

Suicide Prevention Groups, Prayers, Meditations, Exercises, Readings, Books

SUICIDE PREVENTION GROUPS

- **National Suicide Prevention Lifeline**
  https://suicidepreventionlifeline.org/

- **American Foundation for Suicide Prevention (AFSP)**
  https://afsp.org/

- **Suicide Awareness Voices of Education**
  https://save.org/

- **Samaritans**
  https://samaritanshope.org/

- **The Trevor Project (LGBTQ)**
  https://www.thetrevorproject.org/

- **The JED Foundation**
  https://www.jedfoundation.org/

PRAYERS:

Catholic Prayers [2]
https://www.catholicity.com/prayer/prayers.html

Sign of the Cross

In the name of the Father, and of the Son, and of the Holy Spirit.

Our Father

Our Father, who art in heaven, hallowed be thy name. Thy kingdom come, thy will be done, on earth, as it is in heaven. Give us this day our daily bread and forgive us our trespasses as we forgive those who trespass against us; and lead us not into temptation but deliver us from evil.

Hail Mary

Hail Mary,
Full of Grace,
The Lord is with thee.
Blessed art thou among women,
and blessed is the fruit
of thy womb, Jesus.
Holy Mary,
Mother of God,
pray for us sinners now,
and at the hour of our death.

Glory Be

Glory be to the Father,
and to the Son,
and to the Holy Spirit.
As it was in the beginning, is now,
and ever shall be,
world without end.

Apostles Creed

I believe in God, the Father Almighty, Creator of Heaven and earth;
and in Jesus Christ, His only Son Our Lord,
Who was conceived by the Holy Spirit, born of the Virgin Mary, suffered under Pontius Pilate, was crucified, died, and was buried.
He descended into Hell; the third day He rose again from the dead;
He ascended into Heaven, and sitteth at the right hand of God, the Father almighty; from thence He shall come to judge the living and the dead.
I believe in the Holy Spirit, the holy Catholic Church, the communion of saints, the forgiveness of sins, the resurrection of the body and life everlasting.

Nicene Creed

I believe in one God,
the Father, the Almighty,

Maker of heaven and earth,
of all things visible and invisible.
I believe in one Lord Jesus Christ,
the only-begotten Son of God,
born of the Father before all ages,
God from God, Light from Light,
true God from true God,
begotten, not made,
consubstantial with the Father.
Through him all things were made.
For us and for our salvation
he came down from heaven: by the power of the Holy Spirit
was incarnate of the Virgin Mary,
and became man.
For our sake he was crucified under Pontius Pilate;
he suffered death and was buried,
and rose again on the third day
in accordance with the Scriptures.
He ascended into heaven
and is seated at the right hand of the Father.
He will come again in glory to judge the living and the dead,
and his kingdom will have no end.
I believe in the Holy Spirit, the Lord, the giver of life,
who proceeds from the Father and the Son.
With the Father and the Son he is adored and glorified.
He has spoken through the Prophets.
I believe in one, holy, catholic and apostolic Church.
I confess one baptism for the forgiveness of sins,
and I look forward to the resurrection of the dead,
and the life of the world to come.

Guardian Angel Prayer

Angel of God,
my guardian dear,
To whom God's love
commits me here,
Ever this day,
be at my side,
To light and guard,
Rule and guide.

Prayer to St. Michael the Archangel

St. Michael the Archangel,
defend us in battle.
Be our defense against the wickedness and snares of the Devil.
May God rebuke him, we humbly pray,
and do thou,
O Prince of the heavenly hosts,
by the power of God,
thrust into hell Satan,
and all the evil spirits,
who prowl about the world
seeking the ruin of souls.

Act of Contrition

My God, I am sorry for my sins with all my heart.
In choosing to do wrong and failing to do good,
I have sinned against you whom I should love above all things.
I firmly intend, with your help, to do penance, to sin no more,
and to avoid whatever leads me to sin.
Our Savior Jesus Christ suffered and died for us.
In His name. My God have mercy.

PRAYERS WHEN THINKING SUICIDAL THOUGHT'S

a. Prayer for Suicidal Thoughts [3]
https://prayfierce.com/suicidal-thoughts/

Dear God,

Thank you for letting me come to You any time of the day or night with my problem(s). Thank you for being my personal counselor. Right now, I need You. I need to feel You close to me right here and right now. Send your Angels of Protection to guard me. Open my eyes and let me SEE You because right now I feel so alone.

I just want the pain to stop. Everything feels so hard right now. It feels like there is no way out of this, like things could never possibly change. And yet, I **KNOW** your word says that for You, **nothing** is impossible (**Luk 1:37**).

You have come so that I can live my life to the fullest **(Joh 10:10)**, so any thought that I am having contrary to that would not be coming from You. God, You have given me power to take every thought captive and command them to be obedient to You. I exercise that power right now. I command every thought to be obedient to You **(2 Cor 10:5)**.

Help me cast my cares on You beloved God and remind me that You promise I will never be shaken **(Psa 55:22)**. Remind me that greater are You that is in me than the he that is in the world **(1 Joh 4:4)**.

There is no condemnation for anyone in Christ **(Rom 8:1)**, which means there is **no** sin that is too big that You cannot forgive. There is nothing that can separate me from your love **(Rom 8:38)**. No matter what I've done, You love me.

Help me be strong and courageous. Remind me that I am not supposed to be afraid because YOU are with me **(Josh 1:9)**. **Nothing** is unfixable, **nothing** is too far gone. You can turn **ANY** situation around. Lord, please hear my prayers. Your words says "ask and you shall receive" **(Mat 7:7)**. I am asking for your overwhelming peace and comfort. You promise to deliver me from all my troubles **(Ps 34:19)**, please hear my prayers.

God, I need hope. Work in my life. Open my eyes and let me see You working all around me.

In Jesus' name I pray. Amen.

b. Prayers for Suicidal Teens [4] By Kelli Mahoney
https://www.learnreligions.com/prayers-for-suicidal-teens-712263

If You Feel Suicidal:

Lord, I come before You with a heavy heart. I feel so much and yet sometimes I feel nothing at all. I don't know where to turn, who to talk to, or how to deal with the things going on in my life. You see everything, Lord. You know everything, Lord. Yet when I seek you it is so hard to feel You here with me. Lord, help me through this. I don't see any other way to get out of this. There is no light at the end of my tunnel, yet everyone says You can show it to me. Lord, help me find that light. Let it be Your light. Give me someone to help. Let me feel You with me. Lord, let me see what You provide and see an alternative to taking my life. Let me feel Your blessings and comfort. Amen.

If Your Friend Feels Suicidal:

Lord, I come before You with a heavy heart for my friend. He/She is struggling so much right now with the things happening in his/her life. I know You can be his/her greatest comfort. I know You can step in and make a difference. Show me how I can best help him/her. Give me the words and actions that will keep him/her from taking that ultimate step of suicide, Lord. Let him/her see that there is a light at the end of the tunnel and that suicide is not the route to take. Lord, let Your presence be felt in his/her life and let your comfort be what he/she needs. Amen.

PRAYERS FOR ANXIETY [5]

https://www.holylandprayer.com/prayer_for/prayers-for-anxiety/

Prayer For Anxiety- Catholic

Almighty God, You know what I need before I even ask and You know how ignorant I am. Please release me from these anxious thoughts and help me see Your gifts. Aid me in reaffirming my faith so that I can serve You as You first intended. In Your Name, Amen.

Prayer For Anxiety And Panic Attacks

Dear God, I come before You to lay my panic and anxiety at Your feet. When I'm crushed by my fears and worries, remind me of Your power and Your grace. Fill me with Your peace as I trust in You and You alone. I know I can't beat this on my own, but I also know that I have You, Lord, and You have already paid the ultimate price to carry my burdens. For this I thank you, Amen.

Prayers For Anxiety And Worry

Dear Lord, in this moment, I find myself struggling with worries. I know this is not Your will and that You wish me to lay my burdens at Your feet. I know I can turn my cares over to You, who have died on the cross to set me free. I choose to trust in You, Lord, to focus on You, and to leave behind my worries and my cares, as they are nothing in Your light. When I find myself falling to my knees, let it be in front of You, with Your name on my lips, dear God. You will ease my burden and let me live free. In Your Name, Amen.

PRAYERS WHEN AFRAID [6]

https://www.holylandprayer.com/prayer_for/prayer-for-fear/

Prayer for Deliverance From Personal Fear

Heavenly Father, this world You created continues down a dark and lonely road, and the anxiety that constricts my mind continues to grow with it. My focus has drifted away from You to constant worrying and self-doubt. I'm afraid of being a failure. I'm afraid of success, and the responsibilities of that. I'm afraid of criticism from others, and of myself. I'm afraid of being alone, and it haunts me. I'm even afraid of becoming a victim of crime, which can also make life debilitating for me. Bring my thoughts back to You, oh Mighty God! Please be the center of my life, my Rock, my Fortress and my Salvation forevermore. Help me not to stray as the sheep of this world, but to focus my eyes and heart upon You.

Prayer for Withdrawing From Fear, Drawing Closer To God

Fear has pushed me when you wanted me to be led by your loving hand.

Fear has tormented me when you wanted me to enjoy your soothing peace.

Fear has stolen from me when you wanted me to possess that I am blessed with many things.

Prayer for Overcoming Anxiety and Fear In Life

When I feel crushed by my own worries and anxiety, lift my mind and help me to see the truth in all that You are.
When fear grips me tight and I feel I cannot move, please free my heart and help me to take things one-step at a time with you by my side.
When I can't express the turmoil inside my heart and mind, calm me with Your quiet words of love and devotion.
I choose to trust in You, each day, each hour, each moment of my life.
I know deep down that I can cast these cares on You, and that you have taken these anxious thoughts, and by giving your life on the cross, You have set me free.
I choose to trust in You, each day, each hour, each moment of my life.
I know deep down that I live in Your grace, forgiven, and restored by Your sacrifice.

You have set me free, Heavenly Father.

PRAYERS FOR DEALING WITH TRIALS AND TRIBULATIONS [7]

https://debbiemcdaniel.com/2017/08/28/9-prayers-hope-youre-going-storm/

Dear God,

You remind us over and over in your Word that you are always with us. You tell us not to fear and you draw us close into your Presence. You're the only place we find refuge in the storms that surround us right now Lord. You're the only place we can find peace and strength. So we ask you for your words of truth and power to strengthen us in our inner being and life our hearts to you. Thank you for your goodness, thank you that you know the way we take and you have a plan. We look to you today our Lord and Savior, it's your face we seek.

Amen.

Dear God,

Thank you Lord for your word that says you give us the power to come out of this trial "as gold." Thank you that this storm will not last forever, but we're only passing through. Thank you that nothing has taken you by surprise. You know our journey better than we know it ourselves, and you will use this time of testing for good.

Amen.

Dear God,

Thank you Lord that you are Victorious over every trouble and obstacle. Thank you that you have overcome sin, and death, and any evil that we may face today. And because of you, we too are overcomers. We too can have victory, and we can walk strong in your peace.

Amen.

PRAYERS AGAINST EVIL THOUGHTS [8]

https://www.crosswalk.com/faith/prayer/5-prayers-to-pray-against-satanic-attack.html

1. A Prayer to Guard Your Heart

Lord God, Captain of my heart, Satan knows if I follow Your Greatest Commandment – to love You with all my heart, soul, and mind (**Matthew 22:37**) – he is powerless over me. Guard my heart, Lord Jesus, so that it beats for You alone. Don't let me grow complacent toward You or be lured to love anyone or anything more than You. Remove the idols from my heart so that You alone command my allegiance and utmost affections Help me to love and forgive others as You have forgiven me so the enemy can get no foothold through hate or bitterness on my part. Cultivate in my heart Your love that "bears all things, believes all things, hopes all things, endures all things" (**1 Corinthians 13:7**, NASB). Finally, Lord, set my heart on things above, not on earthly things. Help me to remember that You died for me and my life is now hidden which Christ in God (**Colossians 3:1-2**). Increase my longing for heaven so this world holds no power over me.

2. A Prayer to Defend Your Mind

Almighty God,

Cover my mind with the helmet of Your salvation, reminding me constantly that I am Your child and the enemy can't mess with me. Fix my thoughts, Lord Jesus, on what is true, honorable, right, pure, lovely, and admirable. Help me to think about things that are excellent and worthy of praise so Your peace will guard my mind (**Philippians 4:8-9**). Don't let me copy the behavior and customs of this world but transform me into a new person by changing the way I think. Then I will learn to recognize Your will for me which is good and pleasing and perfect (**Romans 12:2**, NLT). Saturate my mind with Your truth so I am convinced that the answers are found in Your Word, not out in the world.

Amen.

3. A Prayer to Calm Your Emotions

Lord, keep the enemy at bay by calming my emotions with the peace of Your presence. Help me to follow Your command and not worry about anything, but pray about everything, with a thankful heart offering up prayers and requests to you so that You can give me that peace that no one can completely understand – a peace that will control the way I think and feel (**Phil. 4:6-7**, CEV). Remind me, daily, that You are the **Only One who can meet my emotional needs** so I don't look to any person for my identity, validation, or for my love tank to be filled. Thank You that You are the God of peace, the God of order, the God who **heals my wounds** and helps me sort through and make sense of life. You are not the God of chaos or confusion. Fill me with Your Spirit so I may express to others only love, joy, peace, patience, kindness, goodness, faithfulness, gentleness, and self-control (**Galatians 5:22-23**).

PRAYER AGAINST EVIL DOERS [9]

https://www.ibelieve.com/faith/prayers-that-focus-on-protection-and-security.html

A Daily Prayer for Protection

Lord God, I pray for Your protection as I begin this day. You are my hiding place, and under Your wings I can always find refuge. Protect me from trouble wherever I go, and keep evil far from me. No matter where I am, I will look to You as my Protector, the One Who fights for me every day. Your love and faithfulness, along with Your goodness and mercy, surround me daily, so I will not fear whatever might come against me. My trust is in You, God, and I give thanks to You for Your love and protection. In Jesus' name, Amen.

A Prayer for Protection Against Evil

Lord Jesus, evil is such a harsh word, and yet Your Word uses it frequently to describe the opposite of good. While we are all capable of sin, I ask Your protection against those who call good evil, and evil good. Guard us from those who scheme against righteousness and from those who twist truth into lies to accomplish their evil intents. May Your angels hover ever near to eradicate fear and fight against dark, spiritual forces we cannot see. Help us cast down every imagination and thought that our enemy tries to use to exalt itself against You.

You dealt our spiritual enemy a fateful blow on Calvary when you died on the cross for us and were resurrected on the third day. While evil still roams, the power of Your name and Your blood rises up to defeat and bring us victory against every evil planned against us. While malicious actions may disturb us, we use the **armor of God** You have given us to stand firm. You will bring justice in due time for all the harm and needless violence aimed at Your children. Until then, we remain in Your presence, aligned with Your purposes, and we look to You as our Supreme Commander and Protector. Help us to avoid temptation, and deliver us from evil, Lord. You are the Mighty One, the One Who will ultimately bring all evil to light. With You, Jesus, we are safe.

A Prayer for Protection from Earthly Enemies

Precious Jesus, You know what it means to be pursued by earthly enemies. And because of Your compassion and understanding, You know the harm we and our families face every day. As Christians and followers of Yours, we will be marked as enemies. Our children need protection from bullies, from misguided avengers, and from false philosophies that attack their spiritual heritage. Fiendish plots pursue our children's hearts daily and try to entice them into harmful practices. Hold our loved ones tightly, Lord, and never let them go.

Command Your angels, Lord, to keep us in all our ways, so that no harm or disaster will come near to our home or our lives. Our trust is not in our ability but in Your stability as our **El Shaddai**. Our weapons of warfare are spiritual, and we look to You for victory. Show us when to speak up, when to listen, and when to act, always aware that You are fighting our battles for us and with us. Teach us to love our enemies, to pray for them, but to resist evil in Your powerful name. We don't fear those who might try to hurt us physically. We are confident in our eternal security. Our fear is a holy, righteous reverence based on Who You are and Whose we have become in You. As Commander and Chief, You will defend us from all earthly enemies. And as long as You are with us, we fear no evil. In Your name, Amen.

PRAYERS FOR FAMILY [10]

https://www.holylandprayer.com/prayer_for/prayers-for-our-family/

Prayer for Family Unity

Lord, I want to thank You for this precious family of mine. For the talents and good things that You have given each of us. Please keep us united, and our bond strong as the days pass. Please guide us, protect us and equip us to do Your will each and every day. Thank You for all that You are, and all that You have given us. My heart is forever grateful!

Prayer for Protection Over Family Members

Lord, I ask for protection and safety over my spouse, my children, my parents, my family members and myself today. Please lead us with Your mighty hands today and always. Deliver us from any enemy and evil that try to hinder our way. Do not let the ways of the enemy blind our eyes. We know that You are for us, so that no one could ever stop us. Please watch over us and guide us all safely throughout this day, so that we may all arrive safely back home, Father. Amen.

Prayer for a Troubled Family Relationship

Heavenly Father, there is a war going on in the souls of many of my family members. I will not be silent about this, and I pray that you will look after them. I also come to you today to pray for the salvation of my family as well. Lord, may my family know You. I pray that they will learn to crave You just as I do. I pray that they will learn to stand strong in the face of trials and tribulations in life. When people knock them down, I pray that they stand up even stronger in You than ever before. I pray that they show love instead of revenge on those who do not agree with them. Give me strength to persevere through any troubles that come my way today. It is time to rise above the sin that comes at me and to that of my family members. It is in Your precious name I pray these things.

PRAYERS WHEN FEELING ALONE [11]

https://prayer.knowing-jesus.com/Prayers-for-Loneliness

A Prayer In Times Of Loneliness And Depression

Lord I feel so lonely at times that I am becoming more and more depressed.. when I am left on my own, with no one to talk to.. and I find that I am trying to fill my life with activities and people – which do not address the root issue of my loneliness or what I am going through.

Lord I know that You have promised to help the afflicted and set free those that are all alone in families.. I pray that You would do just that in my life – so that I may rediscover the joy of my salvation and overcome the depression that sweeps over me so often, when I find that I am on my own and have no one to talk to.

You have promised to help the afflicted and to comfort those that are hurting. Turn Your loving-kindness towards me at this time I pray, comfort my hurting soul and renew a right spirit within me – this I ask in Jesus name,

Amen

A Prayer When Feeing Lonely

How I thank You heavenly Father that You are there all the time and have promised never to leave me nor to forsake me. What a great comfort it is to know that no matter where I am or what I am doing, I can call upon You, day or night.. knowing that Your ears are ever open to my cries for help.

Lord, You know that there are times when I feel so very lonely. I feel that no one I know or seems to understand or even cares. I realize that they all have their own problems and interests - but even those that I am closest to.. do not seem to understand me or show any interest in me.

Lord I know that part of the problem is that I am focusing on myself and my own needs instead of realizing that many other people are probably feeling much the same as me.. and have no one to talk to and no one who understands them.

Help me Lord to turn the eyes of my heart toward You every moment of the day and away from myself.. knowing that only You can provide the fellowship and intimacy that I crave for and that it is You alone Who can flood Your perfect peace into my heart and reveal Yourself to me in a new and special way. Thank You for being my Comforter and Counsellor – I pray that I may draw close to You in a way that I have never known before so that Your comfort and grace may flow through me to others who are going through a similar loneliness – this I ask in Jesus name,

Amen

Prayers For Healing Loneliness

I come to You heavenly Father in a time of great loneliness and pain and pray for Your healing touch upon my life and the sufficient grace to face each day.

I ask for Your comfort and peace, especially during those moments of intense loneliness when I feel so incredibly alone and helpless.

I long for just one person to show a little love and care – and yet the people that I know are too busy with their own lives to notice the intense pain that I am going through. Help me not to be bitter by their lack of love - but rather use it I pray to mold me into the person that I know You want me to be.

Thank You Lord that no matter who forsakes me or displays disinterest in my life – that You are a faithful and ever-present friend, Who has promised never to leave me nor forsake me and that no matter what difficulties or problems I may face... You are always there to love and to care - and to support with Your sufficient grace.

Touch the hearts all those.. who like me are facing loneliness. Comfort all our hearts.; give us the joy of Your Salvation help us all to look to Jesus during those times of loneliness. And I pray that You would help us to grow in grace so that we may be enabled to show comfort and succor to others who are facing times of great loneliness and pain. This I ask in Jesus name,

Amen

PRAYERS OF GRATITUDE [12]

https://connectusfund.org/11-short-prayers-of-gratitude-to-god-for-blessings

Gratitude Prayer

Heavenly Father, thank you that you are the source of all true joy in life. Your word says that everything God created is good, and nothing is to be rejected if it is received with thanksgiving, because it is consecrated by the word of God and prayer. Please help me to receive all the good gifts you give me with thanksgiving and gratitude in my heart. You have loved me and have freed me from my sins by Jesus' blood. To you be glory and dominion forever and ever. Through Jesus Christ our Lord, Amen.

Thankfulness Prayer

Faithful Father, thank you that you can satisfy my every desire and need. Let me give thanks to you for your unfailing love and your wonderful deeds for mankind. You satisfy the thirsty and fill the hungry with good things. Remind me that I lack nothing as your beloved child. Fill my heart with gratitude. You are able to keep me from stumbling and to present me blameless before the presence of your glory with great joy. To you, my God, be glory, majesty, power, and authority, before all time and now and forever. Through Jesus Christ our Lord, Amen.

Grateful Praise Prayer

Generous Father, thank you that, by you, all things were created that are in heaven and that are on earth, visible and invisible. I praise you with all of my heart for your love for me. I thank you for all your wonderful deeds. I worship you for the gift of salvation. I glorify you for my secure, eternal future with you. According to your abundant mercy, you have caused me to be born again into a living hope by the resurrection of Jesus Christ from the dead. Let me continuously praise you. In your powerful name, Amen.

PRAYERS FOR GUIDANCE [13]

https://www.crosswalk.com/faith/prayer/5-prayers-for-guidance-receive-god-s-direction-and-wisdom.html

A Short Prayer for Guidance

Heavenly Father, thank You for Your guidance. Forgive me for getting ahead of Your plans, and help me know when to stop and listen for Your direction. Your ways are perfect, Lord. Thank You for offering gentle grace. In Jesus' Name, Amen. - Kristine Brown

Prayer for Guidance from the Holy Spirit

Lord, I pray you would move the Spirit more boldly in my life. I know that any sin can grieve and diminish the voice of the Spirit, and I pray against the temptation to sin. Help me crave your presence more than I crave sin. Help me grow in the fruit of the Spirit and so walk closer with Yourself. I pray for guidance from your Spirit- let your will and promises always be a meditation of my heart. In Jesus' Name, Amen - Kenny Luck

A Prayer for Guidance When Life is Challenging

Lord, I'm here today with open hands and an open heart, ready to depend on you to help me through the day and all it will bring my way. Help me be like Nehemiah, help me come to you for guidance, strength, provision and protection. As I face tough choices and hard situations, help me remember my beloved God, help me remember that I am Your child and Your representative to the world around me. Help me live today in a

way that brings honor to Your holy name. In Jesus' Name, Amen.
- Charles Stanley

PRAYERS FOR HEALING [14]

https://www.crosswalk.com/faith/prayer/a-prayer-for-personal-healing.html

A Prayer for Personal Healing
God, you know me so well. You created me. You know the number of hairs on my head, and you even know the thoughts conceived in my heart before I ever vocalize them. You've told us to come to you and ask for every need of life. You are Jehovah-Rapha, the God who heals, and you have the final word on my destiny, the number of years I'll live and serve you on earth.

I'm coming to you today as your child, longing to hear from you and asking for your divine healing. There's so much I don't understand about life. But I do know that with one touch, one word, you can make me whole. Please forgive me of my sins, cleanse me of my unrighteousness, and begin your healing from the inside out.

I don't always know what your will is Lord, especially in times like now, when I desperately seek your face. I offer you no promises, no bargains, no deals to exchange for my health. I simply bow my heart before you to tell you the desire of my heart: that I want to spend as many years as I can loving you here, loving others, and wanting to become more like you. However you choose to accomplish that is up to you—and okay with me. If you use doctors to provide healing, give them wisdom to know what to do. Regardless of how you accomplish it, the healing you give is always miraculous. And you deserve all the praise.

A Prayer to Receive Healing

Dear God, I am sick and tired of being sick and tired. I reach forward today, touch the hem of Your garment, and receive my healing. Yes, I want to get well. Give me the faith to walk in freedom and victory. In Jesus' Name, Amen. - **Sharon Jaynes**

A Prayer for Soul Healing

Precious Father, I marvel at the way You love me from immaturity to maturity, from brokenness to wholeness. You don't berate me for my blunders or belittle me for my weakness. You meet me in those places and make me strong. You bind up my wounds so they can heal. You give rest to my heart so it can beat strong again. You are with me. You are God Most High. Do a miracle in and through me, Lord! Heal my soul and make me whole. Make me a Kingdom woman. Help me to live a life totally disproportionate to who I am. May others pursue You when they see what You do through me! In Jesus' Name, I pray. Amen. - **Susie Larson**

PRAYERS FOR PEACE OF MIND [15]

https://www.holylandprayer.com/prayer_for/prayers-for-peace/

Peace of Mind

Dear God I ask for peace of mind. I pray that I am calm, collected and tranquil at all times today. I rest and relax in your presence. I let go of all anxious thoughts. I stop rushing and start praying. I let go and I let God. In Jesus Christ's name, Amen.

Serenity Prayer

God grant me the serenity
to accept the things I cannot change;
courage to change the things I can;
and wisdom to know the difference.
Living one day at a time;
Enjoying one moment at a time;
Accepting hardships as the pathway to peace;
Taking, as he did, this sinful world as it is, not as I would have it;
Trusting that he will make all things right if I surrender to his will;
That I may be reasonably happy in this life and supremely happy with him forever in the next.
Amen.

May I Be At Peace (Saint Teresa of Avila)

May I be at peace.
May my heart remain open.
May I be aware of my true nature.
May I be healed.
May I be a source of healing to others.
May I dwell in the Breath of God.

PRAYERS THROUGH SPIRITUAL DARKNESS [16]

https://www.crossway.org/articles/4-prayers-to-pray-through-spiritual-darkness/

We pray you, God, our Sovereign, Christ, King forever in the world of spirits, stretch out your strong hands over your holy church and over the people that will always be yours. Defend, protect, preserve them, fight and do battle for them, subject their enemies to them, subdue the invisible powers that oppose them, as you have already subdued those that hate us. Raise now the sign of victory over us and grant that we may sing with Moses the song of triumph. For yours are victory and power forever and ever. — Hippolytus of Rome

Now, O Lord, we come and crave aid at your merciful hands that when our enemy comes to bid battle with us, we may by your power and might overcome him, and put him to flight; for we know that he can go no further then you give him leave. . . . O Lord make us strong in you and in the power of your might: put your whole armor upon us, that we may stand steadfast against the crafty assaults of the Devil; for we wrestle not against flesh and blood, but against rule and against power, and against rulers of the darkness of this world, against spiritual wickedness in heavenly things. For this cause, O most sweet Savior, put upon us your whole armor, so that thereby we may be able to resist the prince of this world. —Henry Smith

I cannot, O God, stand in the day of battle and danger, unless you cover me with your shield, and hide me under your wings. You did make me after your image; be pleased to preserve me so pure and spotless, that my body may be a holy temple, and my soul a sanctuary to entertain your most divine Spirit, the Spirit of love and holiness. —Jeremy Taylor

PRAYERS FOR PROTECTION [17]

https://www.praywithme.com/prayers-for-protection.html

The Light of God

The light of God surrounds us,
The love of God enfolds us,
The power of God protects us,
The presence of God watches over us,
Wherever we are, God is,
And where God is, all is well.

St. Matthew, St. Mark, St. Luke, St. John,
Like unto the prophet Jonas, as a type of Christ,
Who was guarded for three days and
Three nights in the belly of a whale,
Thus shall the Almighty God,
As a Father, guard and protect me from all evil.

Grant me Protection

Grant, O Lord, Thy protection
And in protection, strength
And in strength, understanding
And in understanding, knowledge
And in knowledge, the knowledge of justice

And in the knowledge of justice, the love of it
And in the love of it, the love of all existences
And in that love, the love of spirit and all creation.

Let No Evil Befall Us

O God, You are the preserver of men, and the keeper of our lives. We commit ourselves to Your perfect care on the journey that awaits us. We pray for a safe and auspicious journey.

Give Your angels charge over us to keep us in all our ways. Let no evil befall us, nor any harm come to our dwelling that we leave behind. Although we are uncertain of what the days may bring, may we be prepared for any event or delay, and greet such with patience and understanding.

Bless us O Lord, that we may complete our journey safely and successfully under Your ever watchful care.

PRAYERS AGAINST SPIRITUAL ATTACHMENTS [18]

http://www.bandedspirits.com/prayersofprotection.html

Guardian Angel Prayer

Angel of God,
my guardian dear,
To whom His love

commits me here;
Ever this day (Or Night)
be at my side,
To light and guard,
to rule and guide.

Amen

St. Michael Protection Prayer

OPENING PRAYER

Saint Michael the Archangel, Defend us in battle
Be our protection against the wickedness and snares of the Devil
May God rebuke him, we humbly pray.
And do thou, O Prince of the heavenly host,
By the power of God, thrust into hell Satan and all evil spirits
Who wander through the world for the ruin of souls

AMEN

CLOSING PRAYER

In the name of Jesus Christ, I command all human spirits to be bound to

The confines of the cemetery. I command all inhuman spirits to go where Jesus

Christ tells you to go, for it is He who commands you.

AMEN

Circle of Protection Prayer Against Demonic Entity

In the Name of Jesus, I take authority and I bind all powers and forces in the air, in the ground, in the water, in the underground, in nature and in fire. You are the Lord over the entire universe and I give you the Glory for your creation. In your name I bind all demonic forces that have come against us and our families and I seal all of us in the protection of Your Precious Blood that was shed for us on the cross. Mary, our Mother, we seek your protection and intercession with the Sacred Heart of Jesus for us and our families and surround us with your mantle of love to discourage the enemy. St. Michael and our Guardian Angels come defend us and our families in battle against all the evil ones that roam the earth. In the Name of Jesus, I bind and command all the powers and forces of evil to depart right now away from us, our homes and our lands. And we thank you Lord Jesus for You are a faithful and compassionate God.   Amen

PRAYERS FOR STRENGTH [19]

https://www.christianity.com/wiki/prayer/prayers-for-strength-god-give-me-strength.html

Prayer for Guidance and Strength

Dear Lord, I am calling upon you today for
your divine guidance and help. I am in crisis
and need a supporting hand to keep me on the
right and just path.

My heart is troubled but I will
strive to keep it set on you, as your infinite wisdom

will show me the right way to a just and right resolution.
Thank you for hearing my prayer and for staying by my side.
Amen.

For Strength and Wisdom

Thank you, Lord, for being there for me and allowing me to cry out to you in my times of need. It is amazing to me that the Lord of the Universe would take time to listen to me and to care about what I say.

God, there are things happening around me right now that I do not understand. Some of these things make me feel weak, helpless and afraid. Even in the midst of this, I know that you are the Lord. I know that the situation is in Your hand, and I trust You.

I beseech you for strength and for wisdom that I would be able to endure this situation and be able to handle it in a way that would bring glory to Your name. In Jesus name. Amen.

Prayer for God's Strength

Dear God, We thank you for the Power of your Word and your Presence over our lives. We thank you that no weapon formed against us will prosper, for greater are You who is in us, than he who is in the world. We pray that you will cast down every threat and accusation, every abusive word and cruel attack hurled our way. We praise you that nothing is impossible with you, that You are loving and gracious, full of mercy and might. We trust in you alone, to rise up strong on our behalf. Thank you that you are our Defender and Strong Tower, our Refuge and our Strength. Thank you that you fight for us today, and in our weakness, you make us strong. In the powerful name of Jesus, Amen.

PRAYERS FOR GOD'S LOVE [20]

https://prayer.knowing-jesus.com/Prayers-about-the-Love-of-God

Prayer To Be Kept in God's Love In Difficult Times

Heavenly Father, we live in a world where the security we once seemed to enjoy has been eroded right away and so many dark clouds of unknowing seen to be looming on the future's unpredictable horizon - and all that seemed to be so secure and reliable has turned to sawdust in our hands and evaporated like the morning mist.

But Lord we praise Your name that we can entrust our future in Your safe-keeping, knowing that Your love surrounds us and that Your grace is sufficient.. no matter how black the circumstances of life may appear. Thank You Lord that You hold the world in the palm of Your hand, and nothing can snatch us from that secure position in Him.

Thank You that we are accepted in the beloved and loved by the Father and thank You Lord that no danger may overtake any of Your children, that is not permitted by You - and which will not be used to fulfill a just and glorious purpose.

Keep our hearts from unnecessary fretting or worry and in the power of the Holy Spirit may we build ourselves up in your most holy faith.. by praying in spirit and truth and walking the way of righteousness. May we learn day by day to prevent our eyes from focussing on the trials and tribulations that are coming on the earth - and rather help us to look to Jesus, knowing that in all things He is the victor - and we are securely positioned in Him - through time and into eternity...Thank You in Jesus name, Amen

Prayer For Greater Confidence in God's Love

Dear heavenly Father, for most of my life I have tried to earn Your love and gain Your approval.. and whatever I tried to do, never made me feel that I had done enough - in fact the more I tried to get You to love me.. the more I found that I failed You miserably.

And as I look back on the mission trips, ministry activities, times of prayer and the many bible studies I attended.. the more I believed that I must be disappointing to You, because I was not doing as much as I ought to do. Father as I look back at this period of my life, is saddens me to realise what an incorrect perception I had of You.. and Your unconditional love to all Who are saved by grace, through faith in Christ Jesus.

Father forgive me for misrepresenting Your Father-heart of love and thank You for showing me that Your love for me is not dependent on what I can do for You but rests entirely on what the Lord Jesus did for me, on the cross. Thank You that Your approval does not rely on me at all but simply rests on the fact that I believed on the Lord Jesus as my Saviour - and that I am accepted by YOU because of HIM.. accepted in the Beloved because I am a new creation in Christ - clothed in His righteousness and without condemnation.. and all because of Jesus.

Father thank You for this liberating truth, May I never again be drawn into wrong thinking about Your Father-heart of love and may I gain greater confidence and understanding of what my position in Christ truly means - this I ask in the precious name of my Lord Jesus Christ - Who died for me that I might be free from any condemnation.. and receive Your unconditional and everlasting love - Praise His holy name,

Amen

Prayer To Stay In The Center Of God's Love

Help us never to forget that the safest place in a fallen world is to remain in the center of Your will, no matter where we are, who we are with or what circumstances may seem to be looming on the horizon. I pray that I may stay in the center of your perfect will, each day of my life, and that I may walk worthy of my calling and live in a way that is pleasing to You.

May I learn to walk by faith each moment of the day and not be swayed by sight or feelings or emotions.. and may I learn to trust Your word more and more with each passing day, knowing that without faith it is impossible to please You - for it is my heart's desire that in all I do and say, I may be pleasing in Your sight.

Help me not only to do what is good and acceptable in Your eyes, but help me to speak and think aright. May I live in a right relationship with You, walk humbly before You all the days of my life and I pray that I may develop an attitude of grateful praise and thanksgiving. Help me to water all that I say and do with prayer and may my actions and attitudes be rooted in Your love and surrounded by Your grace.

Oh Lord I pray that the words of my mouth be pleasing and acceptable to You, and that my conversation be always full of grace and seasoned with salt - and grant me wisdom I pray, to know how best to answer everyone with whom I come in contact.. in love but without compromise. This I ask in the name of Jesus Christ my Lord,

Amen

Meditations:

YouTube:

- Meditation – Defeating the Thoughts of Suicide

- Guide Meditation for Suicidal Thoughts, Depression, Loneliness, PTSD & Isolation

- Guided Meditation for Detachment from Over-Thinking (Anxiety/OCD/Depression)

- Worship Songs Oreste DAversa (My Personal Playlist when I get into a Funk)

Book Exercises:

EXERCISE 01: BEING MAD AT MY PARENTS - TELL <u>EACH</u> PARENT (and/or CAREGIVER) WHY YOU ARE MAD AT THEM AND GIVE THE REASON(S) WHY YOU ARE MAD AT THEM. Take a piece of paper(s) and tell <u>each</u> Parent (and/or Caregiver) the reason(s) why you are mad at them. When you're done. Go outside, in a safe place, in a fireproof container and take your letter to them and burn it. The purpose of the exercise is to get the "mad" out of you and place it into the paper and then burn the paper, so the "mad" feelings are out of your system (psyche) and sent into the air so they don't come back to bother you any longer. Do this exercise as many times as necessary (Does not have to be in one sitting. Can be over a period of time) Until all of the "mad" is out of you. Fire is a very important basic element, that helps to transmute (change in form, nature or substance) things. Fire needs to be respected when working with it. Remember always being safe when working with fire.

EXERCISE 02: BEING MAD AT GOD (THAT IS IF YOU ARE MAD AT GOD) TELL GOD YOU ARE MAD AT GOD AND GIVE THE REASON(S) WHY YOU ARE MAD AT GOD. Take a piece of paper(s) and tell God the reason(s) why you are mad at God. Yes, this exercise is the same as the one in Chapter 1 but this one is about being mad at God. When you're done, go outside, in a safe place, in a fireproof container and take your letter to God and burn it. The purpose of the exercise is to get the "mad" out of you and place it into the paper and then burn the paper, so the "mad" reasons are out of your system (psyche) and sent into the air so they don't come back to bother you any longer. Fire is a very important basic element, that helps to transmute (change in form, nature or substance) things and needs to be respected when working with it. Remember always be safe when working with fire.

EXERCISE 03: JOURNALING - BUY YOURSELF A NOTEBOOK WITH LINED PAPER AND START WRITING DOWN WHATEVER COMES UP.

Start getting into the habit of writing and you will be surprised what "bubbles up". You will start seeing in your writings, what you need to deal with that has been suppressed, repressed and any painful feelings. These feelings, emotions, events, etc. is the "work" that you have to do, process and heal yourself from. There are professionals to help you with the work (your work), self-help groups and books but ultimately you still must do the work yourself. You don't have to go it alone. There are resources some resources in the back of this book to give you some suggestions.

EXERCISE 04: IDENTIFYING YOUR EMOTIONAL PAIN

In your notebook start to write down all of your "Emotional Pain". This is your personal notebook, and nobody needs to see it. Go to a quiet place and center yourself. Pray and meditation is very helpful. Being is nature is also very helpful. Write the emotional pain that you carry so it can be processed and released from your soul. Start getting into the habit of writing and you will be surprised what "bubbles up". You will start seeing in your writings what you need to deal with that has been suppressed, repressed and any painful feelings. These feelings, emotions, events, etc. is the "work" that you have to do, to process and heal yourself. There are professionals to help you with the work (your work), self-help groups and books but ultimately you still must do the work yourself. You don't have to go it alone. There resources towards the end of the book to give you some suggestions.

EXERCISE 05: BEING ALONE – GET INVOLVED WITH SOMETHING MEANINGFUL.

We don't need to be alone if we do not choose to. Get involve with something meaningful in your life. Be it a local food pantry, animal rescue or whatever resonates with you. You will find that by helping others that need help you will no longer be alone, be meeting new people and have new life experiences. By helping others, we are always helping ourselves. A good place to start is online by going to websites like www.MeetUp.com, Facebook (and other social media websites) or just go to your favorite search engine and typing the words "Local Groups Near Me."

EXERCISE 06: THIS IS A TWO-PART EXERCISE. PART ONE: HAVE YOU EVER FELT LESS THAN? IF SO, DESCRIBE IN DETAIL IN YOUR NOTEBOOK WHAT YOU FEEL. DO PART ONE OVER AND OVER AGAIN UNTIL YOU CANNOT WRITE ANY MORE. PART TWO: FIND YOUR SPIRITUAL PATH OR CREATE YOUR OWN PERSONAL PATH TO GOD. READ BOOKS, ATTEND RELIGIOUS AND SPIRITUAL SERVICES. FIND THE PATH THAT IS RIGHT FOR YOU.

EXERCISE 07: THIS IS A TWO-PART EXERCISE. PART ONE: DO YOU HAVE PAIN, ANGER AND SORROW IN YOUR LIFE? IF SO, DESCRIBE IN DETAIL IN YOUR NOTEBOOK WHAT YOU FEEL. DO PART ONE OVER AND OVER AGAIN UNTIL YOU CANNOT WRITE ANY MORE ABOUT THE TOPIC MENTIONED. PART TWO: WHAT CAN YOU DO TO HELP YOU BE HAPPY?

EXERCISE 08: HAVE YOU EXPERIENCED 'THE DARKNESS' IN YOUR LIFE? IF SO, DESCRIBE IT IN DETAIL AND WRITE ABOUT IT OVER AND OVER AGAIN UNTIL YOU CANNOT WRITE ANY MORE ABOUT IT.

EXERCISE 09: HAVE YOU EVER BEEN DEPRESSED OR ARE DEPRESSED NOW? IF SO, DESCRIBE IT IN DETAIL AND WRITE ABOUT IT OVER AND OVER AGAIN UNTIL YOU CANNOT WRITE ANY MORE ABOUT IT.

EXERCISE 10: HAVE YOU EVER FELT SHAME? IF SO, DESCRIBE IT IN DETAIL AND WRITE ABOUT IT OVER AND OVER AGAIN UNTIL YOU CANNOT WRITE ANY MORE ABOUT IT.

EXERCISE 11: HAVE YOU EVER EXPERIENCED RAGE? DO YOU CONTINUE TO EXPERIENCE RAGE? IF SO, DESCRIBE IT IN DETAIL

EXERCISE 12: DO YOU THINK YOU HAVE ADDICTION(S)? IF SO, WRITE ABOUT THEM IN DETAIL.

EXERCISE 13: DO YOU THINK YOU ARE THE REAL YOU OR ARE YOU FOOLING YOURSELF? DO YOU THINK YOU ARE FOOLING OTHER PEOPLE AS WELL? WRITES ABOUT YOUR THOUGHTS ABOUT THESE SUBJECTS.

EXERCISE 14: HAVE YOU EVER HAD SUICIDAL THOUGHTS? IF SO, WRITE ABOUT THEM IN DETAIL.

EXERCISE 15: ANY ISSUES IN YOUR CHILDHOOD AND/OR ADULTHOOD THAT YOU FEEL ARE NOT RESOLVED IN YOUR LIFE? IF SO, WRITE ABOUT THEM IN DETAIL.

EXERCISE 16: DO YOU FEEL "DAMAGED" OR "BROKEN"? IF SO, WRITE ABOUT IT IN DETAIL.

EXERCISE 17: DO YOU FEEL YOU HAVE AND/OR ARE THERE "CHAINS OF PAIN" IN YOUR FAMILY? IF SO, WRITE ABOUT IT HERE.

EXERCISE 18: DO YOU FEEL YOU HAVE ANY "HOLES IN YOUR SOUL"? IF SO, WHAT ARE THEY? WRITE ABOUT IT HERE.

EXERCISE 19: DO YOU THINK YOU HAVE AREAS IN YOUR LIFE (PHYSICALLY, MENTALLY, EMOTIONALLY, SPIRITUALLY) THAT NEED TO BE HEALED? IF SO, WRITE ABOUT IT HERE.

EXERCISE 20: ARE THERE ANY PERSON(S) YOU NEED TO FORGIVE? DO YOU NEED TO FORGIVE YOURSELF FOR ANYTHING? IF SO, WRITE ABOUT IT HERE.

EXERCISE 21: DO YOU HAVE A HEALTHY LOVE OF YOURSELF? WHY OR WHY NOT? DO YOU LOVE OTHERS? WHY OR WHY NOT? WRITE OUT YOUR THOUGHTS ABOUT THESE SUBJECTS.

EXERCISE 22: DO YOU OWN A PET OR ANIMALS? IF NOT, SPEND SOME TIME A LOCAL ANIMAL SHELTER OR ANIMAL SANCTUARY. WRITE ABOUT YOUR EXPERIENCES AND HOW THE ANIMALS MAKE/MADE YOU FEEL.

EXERCISE 23: GO SPEND TIME IN NATURE. START BY TURNING EVERYTHING ELECTRONIC OFF FOR 5 MINUTES, THEN 10 MINUTES AND SO ON. WRITE ABOUT YOUR EXPERIENCES.

EXERCISE 24: WHAT ARE YOU GRATEFUL FOR IN YOUR LIFE? WRITE YOUR THOUGHTS ABOUT GRATITUDE. WRITE AND WRITE SOME MORE. DO THIS EXERCISE SEVERAL TIMES UNTIL YOU FEEL GRATITUDE IN YOUR LIFE.

EXERCISE 25: ASK GOD FOR HELP IF YOU ARE FEELING SUICIDAL THEN CONTACT YOU'RE YOUR DOCTOR AND/OR MENTAL HEALTH CARE PROFESSIONAL AND/OR CALL THE SUICIDE HOTLINE. IF YOU'RE NOT FEELING SUICIDAL WRITE A LETTER HELPING SOMEONE WHO IS AND MAIL IT TO THE SUICIDE PREVENTION HOT LINE AND ASK THAT IT BE FORWARDED TO SOMEONE THAT **NEEDS HELP.**

EXERCISE 26: WHAT'S YOUR LIFE'S PURPOSE? IF YOU KNOW THEN WRITE WHAT IT IS AND WHAT YOU ENJOY ABOUT YOUR LIFE'S PURPOSE. IF YOU DON'T KNOW YOUR LIFE PURPOSE YET THEN FIND A BOOK OR TWO ON THE SUBJECT TO HELP YOU FIND YOUR TRUE LIFE'S PURPOSE.

EXERCISE 27: WRITE YOUR OWN PERSONAL PRAYER TO GOD. WRITE IT DOWN HERE.

READINGS

The Spiritual Consequences of Suicide
https://www.erinpavlina.com/blog/2007/08/the-spiritual-consequences-of-suicide/

What Are the Consequences of Suicide? Why Not to Commit Suicide
https://www.dadabhagwan.org/path-to-happiness/self-help/suicide-prevention/what-happens-after-suicide/

Suicide and Your Soul
https://ainsliemacleod.com/suicide-and-your-soul/

FOOTNOTES

[1] Hurst, Katherine. "The Law of Attraction." <http://www.thelawofattraction.com/12-laws-karma/>. December 7, 2019.

[2] Author Unknown. "Catholic City." <https://www.catholicity.com/prayer/prayers.html>. December 7, 2019.

[3] Author Unknown. "Pray Fierce." <https://prayfierce.com/suicidal-thoughts/>. December 7, 2019.

[4] Mahoney, Kelli. "Learn Religions." <https://www.learnreligions.com/prayers-for-suicidal-teens-712263>. December 7, 2019.

[5] Author Unknown. "Holy Land Prayer". <https://www.holylandprayer.com/prayer_for/prayers-for-anxiety>. December 7, 2019.

[6] Author Unknown. "Holy Land Prayer". <https://www.holylandprayer.com/prayer_for/prayer-for-fear/>. December 7, 2019.

[7] Debbie McDaniel. "Debbie McDaniel". <https://debbiemcdaniel.com/2017/08/28/9-prayers-hope-youre-going-storm/>.
December 7, 2019.

[8] McMenamin, Cindi. "Crosswalk.com"<https://www.crosswalk.com/faith/prayer/5-prayers-to-pray-against-satanic-attack.html>.
December 7, 2019.

[9] Barlow Jordan, Rebecca. "iBelieve.com".<https://www.ibelieve.com/faith/prayers-that-focus-on-protection-and-security.html>.
December 7, 2019.

[10] Author Unknown. "Holy Land Prayer". <https://www.holylandprayer.com/prayer_for/prayers-for-our-family/> .
December 7, 2019.

[11] Author Unknown. "Knowing Jesus". <https://prayer.knowing-jesus.com/Prayers-for-Loneliness>. December 7, 2019.

[12] Regoli, Natalie. "Connect Us". <https://connectusfund.org/11-short-prayers-of-gratitude-to-god-for-blessings>.
December 7, 2019.

[13] Editorial Staff. "Crosswalk.com" <https://www.crosswalk.com/faith/prayer/5-prayers-for-guidance-receive-god-s-direction-and-wisdom.html>. December 7, 2019.

[14] Barlow Jordan, Rebecca. "Crosswalk.com" <https://www.crosswalk.com/faith/prayer/a-prayer-for-personal-healing.html>. December 7, 2019.

[15] Author Unknown. "Holy Land Prayer". <https://www.holylandprayer.com/prayer_for/prayers-for-peace/>. December 7, 2019.

[16] Author Unknown. "CROSSWAY". <https://www.crossway.org/articles/4-prayers-to-pray-through-spiritual-darkness/>. December 7, 2019.

[17] Author Unknown. "Pray With Me". <https://www.praywithme.com/prayers-for-protection.html>. December 7, 2019.

[18] Author Unknown. "Ohio Researchers of Banded Spirits". <http://www.bandedspirits.com/prayersofprotection.html>. December 7, 2019.

[19] Editorial Staff. "Christianity.com". <https://www.christianity.com/wiki/prayer/prayers-for-strength-god-give-me-strength.html>. December 7, 2019.

[20] Author Unknown. "Knowing Jesus". <https://prayer.knowing-jesus.com/Prayers-about-the-Love-of-God>. December 7, 2019.

BIBLIOGRAPHY

Bloomfield M.D, Harold H. with Felder Ph. D, Leonard. <u>Making Peace with Your Parents</u>. New York, New York: Random House, 1983.

Bradshaw, John. <u>Healing the Shame that Binds You (Recovery Classics)</u>. Deerfield Beach, FL: Health Communications, Inc., 1988.

Bradshaw, John. <u>Homecoming: Reclaiming and Championing Your Inner Child</u>. New York, New York: Bantam Books, 1990.

King, Ruth. <u>Healing Rage</u>. Berkley, CA: Sacred Space Press, 2004

Potter-Efron, MSW, Ph.D., Ronald T. <u>Rage: A Step-by-Step Guide to Overcoming Explosive Anger</u>. Oakland, CA: New Harbinger Publications, Inc., 2007.

Whitfield M.D., Charles L. <u>Healing the Child Within: Discovery and Recovery for Adult Children of Dysfunctional Families</u>. Deerfield Beach, FL: Health Communications, Inc., 1989.

Unknown. <u>The Holy Bible</u>. Authorized King James Version, Oxford UP, 1998.

RESOURCES

Inner Child

- **Healing My Wounded Inner Child: A Journey to Wholeness** –Jan. E. Frazier Perkin
- **Recovery of Your Inner Child** – Lucia Capacchione
- **The Inner Child Workbook** – Cathryn L. Taylor

Soul Retrieval

- **Soul Retrieval: Mending the Fragmented Self** – Sandra Ingerman
- **How to Heal Toxic Thoughts: Simple Tools for Personal Transformation** – Sandra Ingerman
- **Mending the Past and Healing the Future With Soul Retrieval** – Alberto Villoldo, Ph.D

Healing Books

- **God's Healing Scriptures: 240 Prayers and Promises for Healing in the Bible** – Akili Kumasi
- **The Little Book of Energy Healing Techniques: Simple Practices to Heal Body, Mind, and Spirit** – Karen Frazier
- **Chakra Healing: A Beginner's Guide to Self-Healing Techniques that Balance the Chakras** – Margarita Alcantara

Holy Books

- **The Holy Bible** (Old Testament and New Testament) - Christianity

- **The Quran** - Islam

- **The Vedas** – Hinduism

- **Tripitaka** (Pali Canon) - Buddhism

- **Guru Granth Sahib** - Sikhism

- **The Hebrew Bible** (Old Testament) - Judaism

- **Kitáb-i-Aqdas** - Bahá'í

- **Agam Sutras** - Jainism

- **Kojiki** - Shinto

- **Avesta** - Zoroastrianism

THE PHOENIX

The spiritual meaning of the mythical bird The Phoenix. The Phoenix represents transformation and rebirth in its fire. As a powerful spiritual totem, the phoenix is the ultimate symbol of strength and renewal.

I created the symbol below from my own personal rebirth I now gift it to you. Find your own internal Phoenix it's inside of you. It's inside of all of us.

God and I Send you Love! 😊

www.ingramcontent.com/pod-product-compliance
Lightning Source LLC
Chambersburg PA
CBHW062038120526
44592CB00035B/1250